# Writing Poetry

## Shelley Tucker

 GoodYearBooks

*An Imprint of ScottForesman*
*A Division of* HarperCollins*Publishers*

Cover Illustration by Malcolm Farley

Book Design by The Parker Group

**GoodYearBooks** are available for every basic curriculum subject plus many enrichment areas. For more Good Year Books, contact your local bookseller or educational dealer. For a complete catalog, please write:

GoodYearBooks
Scott, Foresman and Company
1900 East Lake Avenue
Glenview, Illinois 60025

 This book is printed on recycled paper

ISBN 0-673-36039-3

4 5 6 7 8 9 MAL 99 98 97 96 95 94 93

# TABLE OF CONTENTS

# Preface

I believe that everyone can compose good poetry and benefit from writing it. Poetry writing is not dependent upon age or academic accomplishment, so adults with little education and children with low test scores are as successful writing poems as people with stronger academic skills. Poetry writing instead relies on a writer's feelings, history, and perceptions, so every person has the background needed to write poems. Because poetry draws on the senses and the senses give deep access to memories and feelings, poetry writing is relevant and interesting. Poetry has fewer rules than prose, so people feel confident when they write.

During the last eighteen years, I have seen thousands of adults and children markedly benefit from writing and sharing poetry. The models in this book have been used extensively with *students* in grades 3–12, in special, regular, and gifted programs, as well as with *adults* writing independently, in poetry workshops, and in university classes. Most of the poems in this book were written by my former students. Their ages are listed under their writing.

Poetry writing is a friend to all writers. During one three-year project, I worked with sixty students; some of them were considered at risk while others were successful in school. Poetry writing was a major part of their curricula. Grades and communication dramatically improved. Suspensions were eliminated. No students dropped out of school.

Part of this power of poetry is that it invites honest reflection and expression. I once had a student who saw a serious accident. Instead of isolating or acting out, he wrote poems about his experience. His poetry helped him remember the details, review his thoughts, express his feelings and understand them. When he shared his writing with us, we heard the truth in his poetry and listened carefully to him. People frequently respond to poetry as we did. There is just as much truth in descriptions of events as in poems about animals and nature. Poetry commands attention and each time writers are heard, they receive clear validation that they are important and that their words matter.

Poetry writing is so engrossing and honest that I have even seen it provide a viable alternative to gang involvement. The appeal of street activities is frequently motivated by the desire to belong, to be heard, and to be important. Students who are given time to write and share their poems form communities right in their classrooms in which everyone is included. By writing openly and honestly, they share their pasts, their beliefs, and their feelings, providing bridges for understanding and empathy.

People write poetry for many reasons. Some write to record their pasts, to validate and to share their memories with family, friends, and classmates. Others write poetry to express feelings and support their own healing. For some, writing poems provides a deepening of their spirituality and their connection with others. Poetry writing expands a writer's creativity, and the principles of poetry enhance prose writing and speech.

Through all of my years teaching poetry writing, I have never worked with anyone who could not write poems. What happens in a classroom in which everyone is interested in the same subject? What changes occur when special education and at-risk students are as likely as other children to win writing awards and get published? What are the benefits for adults who express their thoughts and feelings through poetry? The obvious gains are enhanced creativity and generalization of poetry skills to speech, reading comprehension, and other forms of writing. Equally important, though, are the significant increases in academic motivation, personal expression, self-esteem, and peer respect.

Poetry writing comes naturally. Consider the poems in this book. Some were composed by people with very little education. Many of the authors had never before written a poem. Nonetheless, the poems are articulate and compelling. Each one of us is equipped with the resources to write good poetry—the histories of our lives and the ability to see, think, feel, and hear. When we combine these with the willingness to write, we discover that writing poetry is as natural as walking and talking.

Many people share in the credit for all the work that went into this book. My deepest love and thanks to my husband, Bruce Sherman, and my brother, Richard White. My special gratitude to my mother, Chickie Kitchman, who always values my projects. Thank you to Lauren Wilson, Kay Grant Powers, Diane Adkison, Mary Ellen Cardella, Richard Greenberg, Vicky Edmonds Verver, and Carlos Reyes for sharing their ideas. My gratitude to Natalie Goldberg for her books and wisdom about writing. My appreciation to Seattle Pacific University, the Morningside School, the Private Industries Council, Goodwill Industries, and the public school systems for supporting the connection between poetry and prose, creativity, analytical thinking, and speech.

For many people, writing poetry feels like a great risk. A very special thank you to all of the authors featured in this book who took the risk to write poetry and value what they had written.

Shelley Tucker, 1992

# Introduction

Many of us were taught that poetry must contain rhyme at the ends of lines of a poem. When writing poetry, we had to juggle both sound and meaning, and poems became more like puzzles than art forms for creative expression. As a result, poetry writing often seemed complicated or irrelevant.

Those of us who were taught that lines of poems must end in rhyme were not given complete information about available poetic styles. In many languages, poetry has always been composed in **free verse**, poetry without end rhyme, set structures, or meter (regular patterns of stressed and unstressed syllables). In English, end rhyme was the predominant poetic form from the twelfth century through the middle of this century. In 1855, Walt Whitman published his first version of *Leaves of Grass,* and his collection of non-rhyming poetry became a masterpiece about the American experience. Whitman's work popularized the option of writing poetry without end rhyme, and, during the last fifty years, free verse has become the preferred poetic form in English. This is because free verse allows us to choose which poetic elements we use in our poetry.

If the main definition of a poem is not *a series of lines that rhyme,* what, then, is a poem? A **poem** is a compact piece of writing that contains one or more poetic elements. Rhyme is just one of the many poetic forms. We can easily learn and use a variety of poetic elements to give shape and structure to our poems.

Initially, though, writing poetry may seem like riding a bicycle for the first time. It is sometimes difficult to begin, and, at first, some of the parts of the bike may seem a little confusing and hard to coordinate. Soon, though, with instruction and practice, we come to understand the process and find the balance easily within ourselves. Like bike riding, poetry writing can become second nature and provide us with clear views of new and familiar places.

We also have great freedom in choosing the appearance our poetry takes. A poem may contain one or two words per line, or many. Poets may use no punctuation at all or adhere to the conventions of standard punctuation. Writers can influence the content of their poems by starting each line with a capital letter or by capitalizing the beginning letter of each new thought. Other poets use no capitals at all.

Because the scope of poetry is so broad, some structure, of course, is needed. I developed the models in this book to facilitate the instruction of poetry by teaching a variety of poetic elements. As you work through this book, always feel free to modify the exercises or depart from them completely. The goal of these exercises is to support creativity by giving you some definitions and direction. Once you are on the road, the choice of where to go is yours.

The models and concepts in this book have been used extensively at every grade, pre-school through university and graduate school levels. In the early grades, most of the composition is done orally. At Orca Elementary School, in Seattle, Washington, Vicky Edmonds Verver led groups of six- and seven-year-old students who orally composed the poems on the following page.

## UNICORN

Big, pointy horns
coming out of its head,
the unicorn is magical and nice,
white or pink
and different colors
with wings and a big bushy tail.

They're in Never-Never Land
like Peter Pan,
and they talk like parrots,
or like humans.
They sleep on a stick
like a carousel,
eat purple grass, and flashlights.

Then, with light coming out of their bodies,
unicorns fly to the moon,
and drill holes in it with their horns,
and eat the snowy, green cheese inside.

## DRAGON FLY

A dragon fly
has graceful wings,
big eyes,
and is cautious,
conscious.

He is red,
blue, or black
and flies all around
like a butterfly,
like a helicopter,
or a roller coaster
off its track.

People frequently ask me why very young children are able to compose such wonderful poetry. I believe that children are poets because poetry, like singing, dancing, walking, and talking, arises easily and naturally as an expression of perceptions, beliefs, and experiences. Poetry is a simultaneous connection between the senses and thoughts. It is completely natural for a child to say, "Sadness is white." As children get older, they are steered away from the natural construction of metaphors (comparisons between two unlike things) and toward facts. A definition such as "Sadness is a feeling" comes to replace the metaphor "Sadness is white." It is only then that poetry writing begins to seem difficult.

As writers, our job is to retain and accumulate facts, <u>and</u> simultaneously to regain our wonderment of the universe, our ability to sense sounds in inanimate objects, our desire to draw pictures with words, and our knowledge that allows us to show the connections between unlikely things. Third-graders through adult writers successfully learn and practice the poetic elements in this book by writing their responses; and what wonderful poems they write!

**BLACK**

The color black
is shaped like a rock
and sounds like the wind.

Black is rough
and makes me feel happy.

Black is like the color of night,
the song of the wind,
the month of February,
and a box of shadows.

PAUL FULLER, age 9


Sometimes between the
orange
and the indigo
is the emerald sunset.

Improbable green holding
day and night
apart.

VICKI HAYNES,  Adult


Our times clearly issue a call for the poet in each of us to
come forward. As we write metaphors, we see how things
that once appeared unrelated actually are connected. This
may help us understand and form relationships that are
critical in our interdependent world. Poetry allows us to
draw new pictures and explanations, record our personal
histories, and express our thoughts and feelings in concise
and articulate form.

Have fun using this book. Enjoy and share your writing.
Read your poems or lines from your poetry to family and
friends. Remember the words of Virgil, the Roman poet
who lived 2,000 years ago: "Do not commit your poems to
pages alone. Sing them, I pray you."

# Suggestions for Writing Poetry

Consider these suggestions as you read, write, and listen to poetry:

• Keep a list of ideas.

• Write about things and experiences that interest you.

• Write in your own style to discover your own poetic voice.

• Record all of your thoughts and then edit them.

• Feel free to repeat words and ideas from other poems you've written.

• Take risks. Something that may sound odd in prose may be exactly right in a poem.

• Read your poetry out loud through all stages of your writing and editing.

• Respect what you write. Suspend self-criticism.

• Ask people to give you critical comments in the form of questions rather than suggestions. Suggestions often sound like negative criticism.

• Read other writers' poetry.

• Save the poems you write by collecting them in notebooks or having them bound into a book at a copy store.

# Writing and Editing Poetry

As you write poetry, you will discover methods for composing and editing that work best for you. Here are some suggestions to consider as you develop your writing and editing style.

## Composing

When composing a poem, write down <u>all</u> your thoughts, rather than pre-edit them. When you pre-edit, you compose in your head and then record only selected ideas on paper. This process makes writing unnecessarily difficult. First, pre-editing is time consuming. It is very hard to hold and organize unrecorded thoughts. Second, the sound of the poem is integral to the content. It is generally far easier to hear a poem read aloud than to hear poetry held in your mind. Third, ideas that seem extraneous or inappropriate when first thought, often seem ideal when seen in print.

## Ordering, Deleting, Changing

After recording your ideas, cross out or change unwanted lines (verses). Then, scan your poem for the strongest opening line. Your best opening verse may be half or three-quarters of the way down your page. Put a number **1** next to it, or rewrite the line at the top of the page. Then order and rewrite your other verses.

## Choosing the End Point for a Line of Poetry

Read your poem out loud. Put a slash mark ( / ) at each place you naturally stop. Then, place a mark next to any phrase you want to emphasize and place it at the end of a line. Rewrite your poem, ending each verse with a slash mark.

## Reading

Read your poem both silently and aloud. Watch for "glitches," or feelings inside you that something is wrong. Check these words and phrases. That feeling or hunch may signal that you have made mechanical errors (for example, mistakes in punctuation or spelling) or that you are not completely satisfied with your wording. Go back and pay particular attention to these verses.

# Unit 1—Metaphors

My father used to tell me, "Time is money." When I'm hungry I say, "Pizza is the answer." Yesterday my friend wrote, "Our basketball team's on the road to success." All of these statements are metaphors. **Metaphors**, like the air we breathe, are all around us. They are so common, we usually don't even notice them; but like fresh air, metaphors breathe life into our language.

A **metaphor**, the comparison between two unrelated nouns (persons, places, or things), is one of the most important poetic elements. In the following poem, Vince uses metaphors to make unlikely connections. Notice how metaphors broaden our understanding of the subject of his poem.

**HOPE**

I am hope
as old as earth,
sun and moon.
Yet I feel young,
like a crisp, warm breeze
sweeping down rainy dew fields.

I am the blue of skies,
oceans and rivers,
flowing gentle as rain.
I am hope.
I will not perish,
born of the first man.

VINCE FREEMAN, age 13

# Writing Metaphors

Consider these sentences: "Love is fleeting." "Love is good." The adjective *fleeting* suggests only one aspect of love: time. The adjective *good* provides no picture at all. What happens, though, when "love" is described not by an adjective but through metaphor, the comparison between two different persons, places, and things? Consider the following examples:

Love is a train.
Love is an anchor.
Love is a mountain.

When used in a metaphor, "love" assumes a variety of textures, tastes, smells, sounds, and images that the reader readily associates with the words *train, anchor,* and *mountain.*

It is as natural to compose a metaphor as it is to glance out the window. Look around your room or go outside. Then complete the sentence, "Love is...," by naming any person, place, or thing you see: "Love is a door," "Love is a clock," "Love is the ceiling," "Love is an electrical wire," or "Love is a turtle." Because metaphors are comparisons between any two unrelated nouns, they assume a variety of forms, even when they start with the same word. For example:

Love is a grape, juicy and high overhead.

                    —JAMES McMURRAY, Adult

Love is a mom.          —JAMIL MILES, age 9

Love is a lemon. It can be sweet or sour.

               —KARL HANGARTNER, age 15

Love is the wind, blowing in scared.

               —BILL TAYLOR, age 12

Love is a tree. It always knows where its roots are.

               —KAREN NELSON, age 14

Love is a rug. Sometimes it needs to be vacuumed.

               —DAVID LEE, Adult

Metaphors are bridges. They create images, and, by connecting any two different ideas, persons, places, and things, show things in new ways.

Trees are earth's hair. —CARL McCREARY, age 16

White is time ticking. —NIC SHELTON, age 9

Work is the velcro that keeps reality sticking to you.
—CATHY CHRISTENSEN, Adult

Hair is a broom for your pillow. —SAM WEYER, age 17

Television is the pacifier of teens. —KARL HANGARTNER, age 15

Morning is the topic sentence of my day.
—SUSAN BEAUCHAMP, Adult

A doll is a place to store your love when no one else is around.
—JENNYFER SCHAUBEL, age 12

Food is solidified love. —SHEA JUDD-HUME, age 11

Hands of the artist are branches on omniscient redwood.
—MEL CARTER, age 18

Clocks are electric roosters. —RYAN MACKLE, age 12

Hate is a worn out light bulb. It has no use.
—JENNY MILLER, age 14

A circle is a line that eats its own tail.
—SHIRLENE ROMAIN, Adult

Friends are the mast of companionship.
—JASON SIMONTON, age 13

Doubt is a raging fire lit against the paper of confidence.
—BARBARA JACKSON, Adult

Cars are armor for weary gladiators. —MEL CARTER, age 18

## Activity: Writing Metaphors

To complete this activity, you will write metaphors comparing one noun to another unrelated noun.

**A.** First, write metaphors on the lines below.
**Examples:**   Hair is <u>a broom</u>.
              Love is <u>the wind</u>.

**B.** Then, answer the questions Who? What? Where? When? Why? or How? about some of your comparisons. Note: You do not need to do these metaphors in order.
**Example:**    Shoes are <u>hats</u> (Where?) <u>at the other end</u>.

**1.** Heart of

_____

**2.** Mountains of

_____

**3.** War is a

_____

**4.** Love is

_____

**5.** A school of

_____

**6.** Tears are

_____

**7.** Marriage is

_____

**8.** The ocean is a

_____

**9.** Television is

_____

**10.** The moon is a

_____

**11.** Bottle of

_____

**12.** Kiss of

_____

**13.** Heaven is a

_____

**14.** The army is

_____

**15.** House of

_____

**16.** Cigarettes are

_____

**17.** Ropes of

_____

**18.** Hate is

_____

**19.** Shoes are

_____

**20.** School is

_____

**21.** Tornado of

_____

**22.** Smiles of

_____

**23.** Jaws of

_____

**24.** Hands are

_____

**25.** Mind of

_____

**26.** Teeth are a

_____

**27.** Life of

_____

**28.** Shoulders are

_____

Like smoke from a campfire, a single metaphor often suggests a series of images. Melinda wrote, "The sun is a fireball in the sky," and saw the following pictures unfold from it.

### SUN AND MOON

The sun, a fireball in the sky,
burns a hole in the universe.
Parents take their children to the ocean
to look at the sunset.
And they tell their children,
if you listen carefully,
you will hear the sun
going into the water.
And they say, you can hear
the sizzle of the sun going out
and the rumble of the moon coming up,
waking, to watch over the universe.

MELINDA JACOBS, age 15

Select a favorite metaphor from pages 5–7 and write it at the top of a piece of paper. Then continue writing all of the thoughts that come to your mind, letting your ideas flow freely and unedited. See *Writing and Editing Poetry*, in the Introduction on pages xii-xiv, for suggestions on this composition and editing process.

# Writing Extended Metaphors

Poetry occurs spontaneously in thoughts and speech. One day at lunch, my friend Deborah said, "Do you want some music in your coffee?" Like Deborah, people often think and speak in verse, but how do they move from poetic ideas and conversation to written poetry?

The **extended metaphor** provides a structure for expanding thoughts and speech, gathering content for poems. Choose a favorite metaphor from those on pages 5–7, and write it at the top of a piece of paper. Then list characteristics of the second noun. For example:

Spelling is <u>war</u>
　　　　　　trenches
　　　　　　blow up
　　　　　　bombs
　　　　　　bullets
　　　　　　escape
　　　　　　ammunition

After generating the above list, Matt asked how the characteristic of the second noun, "war," could be used to describe the first noun, "spelling." In the poem on the next page, Matt used his answers to this question for his content.

**SPELLING**

Spelling is war.

> Words fly like bullets.
> Your ears blow up like bombs.

You dig trenches

> on your paper
> for escape.

> MATT LANGHANS, age 12

## Activity: Writing Extended Metaphors

Tony used an extended metaphor, shown below, to gather words and ideas for his poem, "Life Is Dirt." Now you write some extended metaphors.

**Metaphor:**    Life is dirt.

List characteristics of second noun:

Life is <u>dirt</u>
>  mud
>  weeds
>  brown
>  rocky
>  smooth
>  throw it
>  shrinking
>  earth
>  bumpy

Answer:    Life is dirt. Who? What? Where? When?
           Why? How?

**LIFE IS DIRT**

The longer you hang on
the smaller it gets.

Get it wet,
and you've got mud
on your hands.

Take care of life
or it's overrun
with weeds.

Life can be rocky or smooth
and it's great
for throwing at people.

TONY CASE, Adult

# Metaphors About People

Ask eight people what they see when they look at a
tree, and you're likely to get eight different answers,
depending on their points of view. Roots, shade, paper,
agelessness, leaves, home, strength, and work are some
of the many possibilities. By writing poetry in which
you compare yourself to things, you will probably
reflect what you see in the objects back onto yourself.

Sometimes you hear a song on the radio and it triggers a flood of memories. Metaphors work in a similar way. When you read the first lines of Vince's and Vicky's poems below, you recall what you already know about bears, dusk, and dawn. Your memories support your understanding of their poems.

## BEAR

I am a bear,
big and strong.
I feel part of cool rivers
and icy chills.

I sound like a trumpet,
loud and expressive.
The warmth of spring and earth
releases me from the large hole
it prepared to protect me
from the snow season.

I am a bear.
I stand at once young and old,
rough, yet smooth,
loud as a trumpet,
cool as a river,
ice in my veins,
warm as spring.

VINCE FREEMAN, age 13

We are the dawn and the dusk,
we circle around ourselves,
surrounding the hours with ours.

VICKY EDMONDS VERVER, Adult

## Activity: Writing Metaphors about People

Use "I am" (or "we are") to write metaphors in which you compare yourself to animals, places, ideas, and things. Use all of the metaphor starts given here or choose one and expand it. When you write your poem, draw from these metaphors, leaving out some of the "I am's" or "We are's." See the poems on pages 14–16 for examples.

**1.** First, on a separate sheet of paper, write:

I am <u>or</u> we are (and then name something in nature like a tree, a stone, or the sky).

I am <u>or</u> we are (and then name an animal).

I am <u>or</u> we are (and name an age).

I am <u>or</u> we are (and name a color).

I am <u>or</u> we are (and name where you come from or where you live).

I am <u>or</u> we are (and name an object like water, paper, scissors, or honey).

I am <u>or</u> we are (and name an idea like hope, sadness, love, or loyalty).

**2.** Then, after each, tell: Why? Where? When? or How? Here are some examples written by Barbara Jackson:

I am the wind, clean and fresh, rustling you when I move by.

I am a coyote, prowling the woods at night.

I am a flute, air flows through me. My sound pierces the night.

I am ageless, both young and old.

I am green, healthy, smooth, emerald.

I am the sea, expansive and changing and waves, lapping on the beach.

I am sand, flowing through your fingers. Hold me if you can.

**3.** Now, write a poem. You can include new ideas and change parts of your metaphors to suit your poem. Notice how Barbara uses her metaphors in the following poem.

I am a wave lapping on the beach,
from the sea, expanding and changing.
Like a coyote, I prowl at night,
my sound piercing the air.
I am green, like the forest, emerald and soothing.
But come too close and I am sand
flowing through your fingers.
Hold me if you can.

BARBARA JACKSON, Adult

Russell's poem, "Fifteen," and Bruce's poem, "Sailor's Dream," are examples of the power of writing in which people are described through metaphor.

## FIFTEEN

We are 11 eggs
scrambling to make a dozen.

We are the 23 hour day
waiting until October
for the other hour to arrive.

We are 33 ounces to the pound.
(We're dieting, and that's how we count.)

We are fifteen.
One more year till we drive.

RUSSELL ROSENBERG, age 15

## SAILOR'S DREAM

I am water white frozen on deck,
horizontal wind driven snow,
tears on bridge windows
wiped away by black blades
flowing slowly down portholes.

I am water, thick, floating pads of ice,
muddy, brown full of glaciers,
black acrid in coffee
waking the sleepy watch.

I am water stingily yielding barn door halibut,
steamy hot for swabbies' showers
dripping stealthily from a leaky flange
freight train through an unseen hole.

I am water cooling massive machinery,
furious, struggling inside big black boilers.
Let me flow through the blades of turbines
turning the wheel, my price for freedom.

I am water holding the ship in my arms
great smooth rollers like a nursemaid
singing lullabies to sleepy sailors,
and deep waves of green water
white over the bow,
calm at times,
invisible in the night.

> BRUCE SHERMAN, Adult

## Activity: Metaphors About Thoughts and Emotions

You can project human characteristics onto any object.
In doing so, you can use the traits of the things named
to make statements about the characters in your poem.

On a separate sheet of paper, start your poem with one
of the phrases below. Writing metaphors using this
structure gives you the freedom to compare yourself
with a variety of unusual objects such as cars, furniture,
fruits, and vegetables. See J. D.'s poem, on the next
page, for an example.

**1.** In my past I was a....
**2.** In the mirror I am a....
**3.** In my dreams I am a....
**4.** In my stories I am a....

5. In my fears I am a....
6. In my car I am a....
7. In my cat's (dog's) eyes I am a....
8. In my childhood I was a....
9. In my wishes I am a....
10. In these clothes I am a....
11. In the future I'll be a....
12. In my family I am a....

### ISLAND

In my fears I am an island,
surrounded by water,
scarce from everything else.

My age is unknown.
My outskirts are cold.
Water beats upon my shore.

But in my center rests a volcano.
Hot, molten lava
eats away at my greenness
adding land to water.

                    J. D. BROWN, age 16

Notice how Richard develops the metaphor in his poem by using flood-related words: *stream, flowing, river, carries, mud, fertilizer, deposited, downstream.*

### HOUSE FLOOD

In my dreams I am a house in a flood,
the stream flowing
from all my doors and windows.
The river carries me away from the abandoned
yet familiar farm where I made my home.

Now fish tickle the upturned sofa
and frogs leap from teacups on the shelf
and mud, soft and warm,
fertilizes the rug.

I am deposited downstream on a new land
where brightly colored wild flowers
make an oriental tapestry on my floor.

The new tenants are delighted
and eat and sleep outside,
coming in to pick the flowers.

RICHARD GREENBERG, Adult

Jennyfer makes her opening metaphor, "I am a lemon...," textured and believable by using the characteristics of the lemon throughout.

## BITTER

In my dreams I am a lemon in a palace
wearing a yellow dress
that fits close.

Beggars cry for food
at the palace door
but I am too selfish
and give them nothing
but harsh words
and a body of whip marks.

But the regret of being cruel
and not giving food
is hard to carry.
It makes me feel sour
like I'm surrounded by thick, yellow skin.

                    JENNYFER SCHAUBEL, age 12


Metaphors are the heartbeat of a poem. With metaphorical writing, poets are able to eliminate an overused description like, "My summer was fun." Instead, they can say "my summer was a barometer," or "my summer was a glance at the moon." Metaphors create images and comment on how people live their lives, as in the poem by Vince on the next page.

## EAGLE

An eagle is my spirit
standing tall yet endangered,
flying with mighty spread wings
baring my chest and throat above them
as they look down on me
with illuminated eyes.

I soar down to the lake,
go underwater and fly there,
for water is liquid air.

I am part of the mountain,
brought here for you,
but just like the mountains
will I soon be conquered.

I am part of you.
When you fall, I do, too.
You are supposed to learn from me.

But you think all I do is fly around
and that I was born
on the American dollar bill.

                    VINCE FREEMAN, age 13

# Unit 2—Similes

My young neighbor, Myra, says that a shadow is like a tree, happiness is as fun as chocolate cake, and her mom is like an umbrella keeping her dry in the rain. Like Myra, we say and write similes to expand our understanding. In the **simile** "happiness is as fun as chocolate cake," we get a better sense of what happiness means to Myra when we consider the characteristics of chocolate cake: tasty, rich, and filling.

A **simile** is a comparison between two unlike nouns (persons, places, or things) using "like" or "as" to bridge the connection. The examples below show that nouns can be familiar objects, like hands or a circle, or can name human traits, like trust or talk. Jack ends his poem with a simile, and Tyler writes similes naming colors as things.

**REFLECTIONS**

Reflections on iced lakes
Thoughts that wander in your mind
Some surface and reveal another world
The subconscious world
The dream world
That hangs low in winter fields
Like cold, wet fog
                    JACK RUSK, Adult

Black as darkness,
Blue as the sky,
White as paper,
Yellow as dye,
Red as lava,
While the Manta ray glides
Through the shiny, silvery sea.
                    TYLER NEILSEN, age 10


The following examples show how poets can use similes to give their writing a rhythmic quality.

Trust is as ancient as the mountains. —BETH RICHARDSON, Adult
A circle is like a line holding hands. —LAURA MASON, age 14

The teacher's talk, like sandpaper, grated along the outer edges of the class.                              —MARCUS VEDEROFF, age 11

# Using a Simile Instead of a Metaphor

A simile, like a metaphor, is a comparison between two unrelated nouns. A simile functions somewhat differently in a poem than a metaphor does.

A poet sometimes uses a simile rather than a metaphor for rhythm, sound, or syntax. The lines below do not make sense without the word *like*.

The wind swept the town like a broom.
Their ideas ignited like fire.

**Adjectives** are easily included in a simile, extending it and giving it a musical quality.

The night is dark, wet and smooth like a freshly waxed floor.
—CHRIS BUTLER, age 14

Similes are often more subtle than metaphors. A metaphor may be too dramatic or bold for a poem. Consider the differences between the simile and metaphor in each of these sets.

The man is like a tornado.
The man is a tornado.

My skin was like a tomato, red and tight.
My skin was a tomato, red and tight.

## Activity: Similes Using "Like"

**A.** Complete the similes by adding nouns on the lines below.

**Example**:     Night is like a blanket.

**B.** Then, expand some of your similes by answering: Who? What? Where? When? Why? or How?

**Example**:     The breeze is like a whisper (When?) in the morning.

**1.** Television is like

_____

**2.** Summer is like

_____

**3.** Sleep is like

_____

**4.** The moon is like

_____

**5.** Night is like

_____

**6.** Day is like

_____

**7.** School is like

_____

**8.** A dream is like

_____

**9.** Time is like

_____

**10.** Red is like

_____

**11.** Fire is like

_____

**12.** Friendship is like

_____

**13.** Love is like

_____

**14.** The ocean is like

_____

**15.** Hands are like

_____

**16.** Toes are like

_____

**17.** Anger is like

_____

**18.** The wind is like

_____

# Using Verbs in Similes

You can use verbs as part of a simile to create motion in your poetry. Notice how the verbs in the following poems also show pictures.

### JULY 4TH

Yelling like a whistle screams
Expanding like a water balloon
Breaking like a piece of ice
Dashing like a fast car

Watching a display of fireworks
is like the cry
of a great, blue whale.

DAVID WALLACE, age 14

### FEAR

Fear streams like water
and bends like a shark,
expanding like rubber
that's stretched too far.

MARJORIE DUNN, Adult

### TURTLE

feeling like a small fairy
scattering like a worm
waiting like a snail.

MAREK LITTLE, age 10

## Activity: Similes Highlighting Verbs

On the first blank line below, write a topic such as war, love, or summer. Then on the blank lines that follow, complete the phrase, relating it back to your topic. After finishing your worksheet, write a poem drawing from your entries, to develop a theme.

_____ is:

(topic)

**1.** Feeling like_____

**2.** Expanding like_____

**3.** Whispering like_____

**4.** Dreaming like_____

**5.** Scattering like_____

**6.** Turning like_____

**7.** Yelling like_____

**8.** Moving like_____

**9.** Opening like_____

**10.** Waiting like_____

**11.** Streaming like_____

**12.** Rolling like_____

**13.** Blooming like_____

**14.** Dashing like_____

**15.** Dancing like_____

## Activity: Similes Using *As*

**A.** Use *as* to include adjectives in an extended simile. (An **adjective** is a word that qualifies, defines, or limits a noun or pronoun.) In this activity, first you will practice composing similes by writing a noun and a verb to the left of each adjective and a noun to the right. Notice how Martin uses similes in his poem, shown at the bottom of this page.

**1.** _____ as strong as _____

Her hands grasped as strong as steel.

**2.** _____ as full as _____

The man smiles as full as the moon.

**3.** _____ as rough as _____

Their attitudes were as rough as sand.

**OCEAN**

An ocean is as round as an arc,
as broad as the sky,
as deep as our memories,
as inviting as a friend
waving hello.

MARTIN ROSEN, age 15

**B.** Now, compose your own similes. Write a noun and a verb on the line to the left and a noun on the line to the right of each adjective listed below.

**Examples**:  My reflection moved as swift as the wind.
Hope is as ancient as the sea.

1. _____ as loving as _____

2. _____ as ancient as _____

3. _____ as gentle as _____

4. _____ as blue as _____

5. _____ as deep as _____

6. _____ as exhausting as _____

7. _____ as round as _____

8. _____ as mean as _____

9. _____ as brave as _____

10. _____ as sharp as _____

11. _____ as magical as _____

12. _____ as strange as _____

13. _____ as sudden as _____

14. _____ as strong as _____

15. _____ as young as _____

Similes are often subtle and musical. In Bianca's poem below, the moon is like a tiger's eye. A dream is compared to a foreign language tape in Vicky's poem, "Continuous Loop."

When I lie in my bed,
I feel the wind closing the house
in a white veil,
getting tighter and tighter,
and the moon an eye
looking at the wind like a tiger.

                    BIANCA PERLA, age 13

## CONTINUOUS LOOP

Sometimes words come in my head while I sleep.
Disconnected phrases float through like a foreign language tape
that plays on a continuous loop.
Stuck there, I dream dismembered sentences
written on a blank blackboard
where chalk falls to dust before I wake.
Memories mold to morning's madness.
Did I forget something important?

                    VICKY EDMONDS VERVER, Adult

Similes show how things and experiences that at first seem different may really be similar.

## DON'T FORGET TO FLOSS

Therapy is like dental floss.
Everyday you clean
out the crud crammed in the cracks,
and then you go eat
a hot fudge sundae
with your nuts,
your bananas,
and a little caramel sauce.
You could work all day on that one
and still miss a problem area or two.

Ten or twenty years down the road,
you find you got yourself
some permanent damage.

Then it's time to call in the big guns,
examine your roots.
You may need a canal or a bridge
to get out of this one in one piece.

Then what do they tell you,
Don't forget to floss.

VICKY EDMONDS VERVER, Adult

## BLUE

Blue sounds like the wind
and is shaped like a diamond.
Blue looks like a dancing filly,
is the song of beauty,
and a big, blue box of love.

MARA HAMBORG, age 9

# Unit 3—Personification

The word *personification* helps us remember what personification means, making things seem like people. Personification is so powerful that even one line can create a vivid scene. Barbara Turner wrote, "Honest potatoes empty their pockets on the plate." Suddenly, we have a picture of potatoes that seem like people wearing pants and coats.

**Personification** is the assigning of human traits to things, colors, qualities, and ideas. There are many ways to personify things so they seem human. Martin writes about stones as though they are people having thoughts, giving answers, and wearing clothes.

## STONES

Stones know the answers.
Their roundness is like hands cupped in prayer.

They dress carefully,
sometimes wearing moss cloaks.

There are messages inside of stones,
deep memories of mountains and oceans.

So sometime, ask a stone what it knows.
Tap it softly like a drum
or throw it gently on a pond
and watch its answer appear
as sound waves across the water.

MARTIN ROSEN, age 15

Personification allows you to add a human dimension to any object, color, quality, or idea. You know that a car has four tires, an engine, and a steering wheel, but what happens when the car is personified? Consider the following examples:

The happy car cheered when it greeted the tow truck.

Their car cried out for more gas before it went to sleep on the side of the highway.

With personification, your view of the car broadens as it takes on a variety of human traits. Personification also creates images and humor in poetry.

Trash *rallied* around the dumpster *cheering* for the garbage man.
—BETH ASHLEY, Adult

*Romantic* trucks *kiss* other cars' bumpers.
—RICHARD SMITH, age 12

The stapler removers *eat* with metal *teeth*.
—ANNA STEIN, age 14

Hole punch *chuckles*, paper circles dripping from its *mouth*.
—LAINIE RILEY, Adult

The sparkle of rain is a sky *watching* over me.
—MALINA BASH, age 11

Candles *cry* wax *tears*.        —BRIGIT McSHANE, Adult

My *happy* fork *dances* through the macaroni and cheese.
—JOSEPH ZUCKERMAN, age 16

The rain *typed* a letter on my window sill.
—BETH RICHARDSON, Adult

The *fearful* lightning was banging against the ground with sparkling blows.        —EZRA MILLER, age 9

# Ways to Write Personification

Personification is perhaps the modern-day equivalent to rhyme. As little children, when you heard rhyme you probably knew you were listening to poems. In a similar way, personification makes your writing poetic. With personification you expand the scope of your topics, and frequently have fun while you write. Consider using personification in your poems in any one of these five ways. (Note: pages of related worksheets are listed under the examples.)

**1. Use verbs that name human actions.**

Love *remembers* the good times.
Cats *tango* in the streets.
(pages 37–39)

**2. Write with adjectives that generally are used to describe people.**

The *embarrassed* clock covered its face with its hands.
*Worried* peas glance at the boiling water.
(pages 41–42)

**3. Refer to object, ideas, qualities, and color using personal pronouns.**

I called out to the ocean, and *she* waved back to me.
I coaxed my motorcycle, but *he* still wouldn't start.
(page 43)

**4. Give things human body parts.**

The tree stretched its *legs*.
Our watches shook *hands*.
(page 44–45)

**5. Construct a complete personality for an object by discussing its friends, home, or job.**
Judgment *works* at the *bank*.
Green's *best friend* is envy.
(pages 47–48)


In the following poems, Mel and Carolyn use verbs that name human actions, so that trees, skyscrapers, and the moon move as people.

### JONATHON STUDLEY

I'm so big and cool,
when I walk, dogs blow trumpets.
When I pass, trees <u>salute</u>.
When I roam, leaves <u>step</u> to one side.

I'm so macho, when I skateboard,
skyscrapers <u>jump</u> out of my way.
When I get to my neighborhood,
the block <u>rolls</u> out the carpet.

When I pass my friends,
the gang bows down to grovel my Converse.
When I step up to my front walk,
the concrete <u>plays</u> a tune.

When I get to my house,
Gotdang, man,
I've got to take the trash out,

Again.

                    MEL CARTER, age 18

**A STORY UNTOLD**

The moon <u>creeps</u>,
in the midnight air.
It <u>speaks</u>,
of fears and terrors.
It <u>sings</u>,
of a single soul.
It rings,
of a story untold.

CAROLYN HART, age 15

## Activity: Personification Naming Human Actions

**A.** Personify things, ideas, and qualities by writing a *human action* next to each object listed below.

**Examples**:   The moon <u>winked</u>.
My refrigerator <u>laughed</u>.

**B.** Then, expand some by answering Who? What? Where? When? Why? or How?

**Examples**:   Dirty clothes <u>got up and walked</u>
(Where?) <u>into the laundry room</u>.
The sun <u>smiles</u> (When?) <u>in the morning</u>.

**1.** Oceans

_____

**2.** Waves

_____

**3.** Cars

_____

**4.** Wheels

_____

**5.** Trash

_____

**6.** Birds

_____

**7.** Machines

_____

**8.** Heart

_____

**9.** Math

_____

**10.** Sun

_____

**11.** Hands

_____

**12.** Hats

_____

**13.** Necklaces

_____

**14.** Homework

---

**15.** Dogs

---

**16.** Glasses

---

**17.** Sound

---

**18.** River

---

**19.** Moon

---

**20.** House

---

**21.** Eyes

---

**22.** Flashlights

---

**23.** Staplers

---

**24.** Computers

---

The words *gentle*, *loyal*, and *cautious* are generally used to describe people. In the poems that follow, the writers use these words instead to give the wind, time, and the moon new dimensions. In Joni's poem, notice how just two words—*cautious moon*—show a picture of an object with movement and feeling.

### WIND

The *gentle* wind whispers,
Put on your coat.

JERRY GALLAGHER, age 9

### TIME

Time is *loyal*.
She doesn't understand
why people say she always runs out.

Time is *amused*
when people treat her as a commodity,
like a spice missing from the rack.
*Honey, when you go to the supermarket tonight,*
*will you get me some parsley, sage, and time?*
*I'm all out of time.*

DORIS CHIN, Adult

## MOON

The *cautious* moon remembers,
but only tells her story at night.
Once when she was *young,*
she jumped out right in the middle of the day.
But the sun was too strong
and it bleached her egg-shell white.
Now, the moon moves slowly in the midnight sky
and *wears* layers of clouds for clothes.

JONI SINGER, age 16

## Activity: Describe Things as People

**A.** In this activity, you will write about things using adjectives that usually describe people. Write the name of an object next to the adjectives listed below.
**Example**: Honest <u>machines</u>.

**B.** Then, expand the expression by answering Who? What? When? Where? Why? or How?
**Example**: Talking <u>hands</u> (What?) <u>speak about</u>
friendship.

**1.** Happy

**2.** Thoughtful

**3.** Mean

_____

**4.** Caring

_____

**5.** Loyal

_____

**6.** Dumb

_____

**7.** Lying

_____

**8.** Smart

_____

**9.** Honest

_____

**10.** Lazy

_____

**11.** Sulky

_____

**12.** Sneaky

_____

# Personification Using Personal Pronouns

Poets personify things by using feminine pronouns
(*she, her,* and *hers*) and masculine pronouns (*he, him,*
and *his).* In the poem below, Al refers to the brook as
*she* and *her.* The brook seems almost human as she
goes on with her chores, not noticing her guests who
want her to stop and visit.

**TIMBERDOODLE**

The mischievous clouds erased the moon from the sky
Writing in their own darker subjects,
Shutting out the light that lead me
Down the path
Occupied in inviting me to explore
Its descent to the brook below.

Now the leaves of trees, shrubs, and grasses
Tenderly guided my way
As I wandered on.

When I reached the brook, she was too busy to greet me
Like one rushing on with life
Oblivious to the guest that calls her away
From daily chores.

AL BANDSTRA, Adult

## Activity: Giving Things Life

First, choose an object. You may want to use a thing from the list below. Then, on a separate sheet of paper write a poem about it, referring to it as a person.

| | |
|---|---|
| river | flowers |
| ocean | computer |
| heart | motorcycle |
| house | tree |
| car | friendship |
| boat | gun |
| honesty | school |
| love | war |

## Activity: Personification Using Human Anatomy

On a separate sheet of paper, use the words below in reference to things. See the poems on the next page for examples.

| | |
|---|---|
| ears | eyes |
| mouth | nose |
| arms . | knees |
| fingers | hands |
| hair | toes |
| teeth | skin |
| muscles | wrist |

What happens, in the poems below, when things are given cheeks, arms, and eyes? Suddenly, a car dances, a wave hurls, and a traffic light sees.

## CAR CACOPHONY

On Friday nights
cars drool and dribble from over-stuffed bellies.
They dance during rush hour
*cheek to cheek* on freeways
and cavort on city streets,
over-eating and under-drinking.

Depressed clutch pedals shriek for oil's ointment.
Tires howl, spanked by broken nails.
Wheels squeak at the sight of curbs.
Brakes squeal their protest to motion
as headlights anxiously read road signs
looking for more gas.

> KATHRYN CAMPBELL, MICHELLE McKENZIE,
> AL CHASE, LAINIE RILEY, BRUCE SHERMAN
> VICKY EDMONDS VERVER, SHERMAN MARTIN,
> TIP TOLAND, Adults

Surfing—The wave picked me up in her *arms*
and dumped me on the beach.
> JON SINGER, age 16

The stoplight
blinked its *eyes* at me.
> JOSH PRESCOTT, age 9

Jamie's and Kathryn's poems below show how things come alive in poetry when given personalities.

## RED

Red works on the points of the sun,
and goes into the mist in the sky
for a vacation.

JAMIE SOHL, age 12

## JUDGMENT

Judgment used to hop on my lap
without waiting to be asked,
and he weighed so much,
he squished my thighs.

Judgment works at the bank
where he counts what goes in and out,
all day measuring each its value,
deciding what is enough.

When judgment goes skating,
he's stiff and falls down a lot,
simply because he is scared
of not looking good.

I decided that besides being heavy,
judgment did not see me clearly
for who I really am,
and though I haven't discarded our friendship
I asked him to sit in his own chair
in front of me,
so I can see him clearly.

KATHRYN CAMPBELL, Adult

## Activity: Giving a Thing a Complete Personality

---

**A.** Choose a thing, color, or quality below to personify.
Write your topic on a separate sheet of paper.

### 1. Human Emotions and Traits

| | |
|---|---|
| love | fear |
| friendship | envy |
| worry | passion |
| bravery | respect |

### 2. Colors and Textures

| | |
|---|---|
| red | yellow |
| white | turquoise |
| blue | salmon |
| opaque | transparent |

### 3. Human Anatomy

| | |
|---|---|
| heart | eyes |
| liver | lungs |
| knees | feet |
| hands | fingers |

### 4. Nature

| | |
|---|---|
| trees | sea |
| wind | sky |
| stones | sand |
| breeze | clouds |

### 5. Things

| | |
|---|---|
| cars | doorknob |
| refrigerator | stove |
| plastic | keys |

**B.** Now, give the thing you chose a personality by providing some more information about it. Describe, for example:

- where it lives

- its favorite colors, clothes, food, holidays

- its job, hobbies

- its friends and relatives

- where it goes on vacation

- its memories and emotions

- its dreams and desires

- problems it has

- the way it moves

Personification allows a writer to create pictures in which things seem completely human. In the poem below, Chickie uses personification to make a stapler talk.

**STAPLER**

The stapler spanks the paper
crying out like a parent,

This is my duty.
It hurts me more
than it hurts you.

CHICKIE KITCHMAN, Adult

Personification draws pictures and shows new connections between people and things.


The clouds reached out
with long, thin arms
and covered the moon
from our view.

PETER BENNETT, age 9


The ocean devours
the logs on the beach
with little rock teeth
and a big sandy tongue
swallowing back with the tide.

VICKY EDMONDS VERVER, Adult


My sweat incriminates me
as it finds its way into rivers,
streaming over my temples
and down my neck,
absorbed into the spray starched collar
of my interview.

TIP TOLAND, Adult

# Unit 4—Imagery

In poetry, you can create **imagery**, or pictures, easily and effectively. When you use metaphors and similes, the reader automatically sees pictures of the things being compared. Personification shows pictures in a similar way. Because the objects being named are compared to people, the reader sees the human characteristics transferred onto the object. Read "My fork dances through the spaghetti," and the prongs of the fork suddenly seem like legs.

This chapter covers two other ways to create imagery in your poems: **1)** by using action verbs and **2)** through writing with close attention to detail. Notice how easy it is to see Vince's swamp in the poem below. He draws a picture by using vivid action verbs, such as *hovering* and *swoops*, and by carefully describing the birds, sounds, and shadows.

### SWAMP

Hovering over the hot, damp swamp
a small, red bird swoops down
on an insect.
Light blue shades of atmosphere
and smoldering heat fill the air.
Whooping sounds of wild birds
awaken the swamp
from its lazy, midday dreams.

Sun fades away
into the back pocket of earth.
Misinformed shadows
petrify the man in the bush who awakens
knowing lazy sun and heat
have beaten him with a sleepy stick.

Sun peeks around the corner,
spreading arms in all directions,
driving night and darkness away.
A little, red bird appears
hovering over the swamp
and swoops down
on an insect with illuminated wings.

           VINCE FREEMAN, age 13

# Creating Images with Action Verbs

Poets can *show* feelings, scenes, and experiences or *tell* about them. The sentence "I laughed so hard I cried," shows a picture. The sentence "I was happy" tells about the event.

The verbs poets use in their writing, in part, determine whether readers see pictures or hear about them. **Action verbs** create pictures in the mind because they show the motion. There are two groups of verbs, however, that frequently *tell* rather than *show* imagery. These are called **auxiliary verbs** and **linking verbs**, and they express a state that is *experienced* rather than *seen*.

Look at the following pairs of sentences. The first one in each set *tells* about an emotion or scene while the second sentence uses an action verb to *show* a picture of it.

*Tell* : I was sad.
*Show* : I wept.

*Tell* : He is angry.
*Show* : He throws all his books on the floor.

*Tell* : They seemed friendly.
*Show* : They came over and introduced themselves to us.

*Tell* : They were considerate.
*Show* : They gave us some of their cake.

## Linking Verbs and Auxiliary Verbs

Below are lists of linking verbs and auxiliary verbs. A **linking verb** connects a subject to a modifier as in "We are happy." An **auxiliary** or **helping verb** is used in conjunction with another verb as in "She is running." Both types of verbs express a state that is experienced rather than a state that is seen.

| Linking Verbs | Auxiliary Verbs |
| --- | --- |
| am | am |
| is | is |
| are | are |
| was | was |
| were | were |
| will be | has |
| can be | have |
| may be | had |
| has been | be |
| have been | been |
| had been | do |
| should have been | does |
| could have been | did |
| would have been | can |
| should be | could |
| could be | should |
| seem | would |
| feel | will |
| become | must |
| remain | may |
| appear | |

## Activity: Imagery Through Action Verbs

Rewrite each sentence on the line below it to *show* a picture. Do not use the following verbs: *am, is, are, be, been, was, were, being, seem, seemed, feel, felt.* Keep the same meaning, as in the first example, or give an illustration, as in the second example.

**Example**: *Original sentence* : The students were cold.
*Rewritten* : The students shivered in class.

**Example**: *Original sentence* : He is excited.
*Rewritten* : He leaves today for Hawaii.

**1.** He is lucky.

_____

**2.** I am happy.

_____

**3.** The bus was hot.

_____

**4.** They were angry.

_____

**5.** Summer is fun.

_____

**6.** I feel great.

_____

**7.** My life is good.

_____

**8.** They were tired.

_____

**9.** You seem jealous.

_____

**10.** I am lost.

_____

**11.** They are brothers.

_____

**12.** She seems honest.

_____

## Activity: Picture It with Verbs

Select a topic from the list below and write a poem showing a picture of it. For this exercise, use as few of the following verbs as possible: _am, is, are, was, were, be, been, being, seem, seemed, feel, felt._ See Mickey's and Chris's poems on the next page for examples.

| | | |
|---|---|---|
| love | guilt | hate |
| loyalty | jealousy | sadness |
| courage | hope | fear |
| anger | honesty | forgiveness |

Mickey writes about loss. She shows the pain through her choice of verbs: *grasp, drops,* and *hurts.*

Riding on a bus
We see a deer.
As we pass
She lifts her head.

In my mind I grasp her pain.
She drops her head
And shows her life is going.

A lady there
Also hurts
For the life lost
Of something wild.

MICKEY STURZA, age 18


Chris's poem is about struggle, and his verbs support and develop his theme.

The wall east of me is strong and tall.
It stretches pole to pole.
I mean to get to the other side.

I hammered and blasted and chiseled
Without making a dent.
I climbed and clawed and vaulted for years
And always slid down.

At last, I admitted my problem and headed west
Thankful that the world is round.

CHRIS McLEOD, Adult

## Activity: Movement with Verbs

First, make a list of action verbs. Then, on a separate sheet of paper, write a poem beginning many of the lines with them. When you read the poems below and on the next page, notice the placement of the verbs in them. Verbs that start lines provide direction and momentum. Each one gives a snapshot of the action it names.

### SEA

Collect the flat stones
that linger on the beach.
Launch each skipping
against the waves.

Liberate the pebbles
from the sandy walls.
Roll them through your fingers.
Plunk them into the water.
They will splash your face.

Visit with the limpets.
Match-up the sea stars.
Caress the anemones.
Listen to the seashells.

Touch the sunset.

LISA STUEBING, Adult

Walk slowly by the stream and
hear the hum of the trees.

Look carefully into the sky and
wink back at the stars.

Linger in the morning and
collect your dreams.

Go slowly, go slowly, go slowly.
Take time by the hand and dance.

JESSIE HIGGINS, age 16

## Creating Imagery Through Detail

Poets create pictures of people, places, and things by
writing *detailed accounts* of texture, movement, sound,
smell, color, size, function, shape, and light. In the
poem below, Mel carefully describes the ocean by
writing about everyday things like the quality of light
and the movement of a tree, and readers vividly see
the scene as though looking at a picture.

**THE OCEAN**

The ocean shifts under the moonlit sky
Waves ripple and churn
White caps pitch.
Golden streaks of reflected light flash
in the warm moonlight.

Wind blows onto sandy shores.
Rocks and driftwood,
glass and seashells heap
on the shoal.

Palm trees swish their heads
back and forth,
their spiked hair waving a hello.

MEL CARTER, age 18

## Activity: Writing with Detail

First, choose either a place or a thing from the lists
below. Then, on a separate sheet of paper, carefully
describe your topic, paying close attention to detail. For
this exercise, *do not* include feelings. Instead, rely on
details to set the mood, as Fred did in his poem on the
next page.

### Places:

| | |
|---|---|
| the ocean | a ball game |
| a lake | an institution |
| a street | a house |
| a room | a store |
| a concert | a lake |

### Things:

| | |
|---|---|
| car | book |
| toy | motorcycle |
| computer | fruit |
| tree | clothing |
| telephone | food |

## COVE FACING EAST

If I were to find a land that I liked
it would be beautiful
with waterfalls and streams
that go to the sea.

There would be sand which is warm
when you walked in it,
a deer grazing in a field,
birds that would sing in trees.

At the top of a mountain
would be a cabin by a cliff.
But the magic of this island
would be a cove facing east.
There would be an old fishing dock there.

And, sometimes, in the middle of the day,
The whales would swim by.

FRED THIEME, age 17


Delphine writes a detailed description and the reader
can easily see her scene, as though watching a movie.

## JOY

I wake this morning feeling joy.
My sandy cat drools in my face.
Smell the coffee brewing.
Hear sounds of soft slippers.
I see my friend's smile.
My friend loves me toothless.

DELPHINE BOWERS, Adult

# Unit 5—Alliteration

**Alliteration** is the same beginning consonant sound in two or more words close together. It is like rhyme at the beginnings, rather than at the ends, of words. We hear it in advertisements, political slogans, and nursery rhymes. The rhythmic quality of alliteration engages the ear and often shows us the humor in language.

Jovial, jolly Santa jammed in the chimney.
Big baboon bit the banana.
Mad Mickey Mouse made Minnie Mouse do math.

JENNY MILLER, age 14

Hands are used for handling.
Noses are meant for nosing around.

TIP TOLAND, Adult

### SCHOOL OF LOVE

A school of love teaches you how to love and care,
as you learn your lovabets from a–z.

A school of love teaches you different ways to spell,
as you put your words in lovabetical order.

TRENITA HARRIS, age 11

Repeated sounds have serious connotations too. Say
the sounds of the following letters aloud slowly: *d, h, b,
w, m,* and *s.* These sounds may suggest an emotion, a
musical instrument, or even a place. Students often say
that *d* reminds them of banging and doom; *h,* lightness,
a breathy, airy feeling; *b,* a drum; *w,* softness and
whispers; *m,* humming, whirling, and a clarinet; and *s,*
quiet, secretiveness, and a song.

The poems below repeat sounds. Notice how the
sound of alliteration affects the meaning of each poem.

Baseball gloves
and bats and caps
were raised in salute,
as the umpire called,
Batter up!

JON SINGER, age 16

### THE MOON IS A MAGICIAN

The moon is a magician
with a wound filled of light.
Air birds and rabbits pop and fly out
of its black, tall, shiny hat.

Moon magic is private magic.
Sometimes, it's a big white ball
swirling spokes and colors through the trees
and many leaves that cover the grass.

Then the moon brings out its magic wind
to blow away the sparkling leaves.

JOVAN LEWIS, age 11

Wet, cool earth's watering smells,
welcomes the new day rising.

JENNYFER SCHAUBEL, age 12

## Activity: Writing with Alliteration

Write at least *five* alliterative words next to each letter listed below. Write unrelated words or words that form sentences. If you write sentences, include some words that are not alliterative.

**Examples**:  **f**  frame, fabulous, fragrant, fig, fish
                 **b**  The big bear and the baboon bit bananas and pears.

**1) b**

---

**2) c**

---

**3) d**

---

**4) f**

---

**5) g**

---

**6) h**

---

**7) j**

---

**8) k**

---

9) l

_____

10) m

_____

11) n

_____

12) p

_____

13) q

_____

14) r

_____

15) s

_____

16) t

_____

17) v

_____

18) w

_____

19) y

_____

20) z

_____

Repeated sounds have particular connotations. What is the connotation of the sound of *j*? In Mel's poems, below, it is humor.

### JOE AND JOHNNY

Johnny's jam jugs hold juice.
Joe's giant jars hold jugs.
Does Johnny's jug jar Joe's mind?
Or does Joe's jar jug Johnny's?

Well, to jar juice jugs devalues jars.
But to jug jam jars gyps jugs.
All in all, whether they jar or jug,
Joe and Johnny are in quite a jam.

### TONGUE TWISTER

Johnny Jokes, a jolly jester,
played jokes on all the lads.
But one fine day, he played a joke
which ended up quite sad.

He tripped a man in long frock coat
and slopped him up with grease.
Then got locked up for drowning
LA's Chief of Police.

MEL CARTER, age 18

# Unit 6—Onomatopoeia

When Caitlin Wilson was two years old, her conversation about ducks naturally included their sound, "Quack, quack." She knew that the "bow wow" of a dog and the "meow" of a cat were integral parts of these animals. Caitlin spoke using **onomatopoeia**, the formation of words that sound like, or suggest, the objects or actions being named. Like Caitlin, advertisers, children's authors, and cartoon writers use onomatopoeia because these words engage the ear and stress the importance of expressive sounds.

## ONOMATOTODAY

In the morning
>yawn, stretch

to the bathroom
>scratch, blink

in the shower
>scrub, splash

to the closet,
>whisk, rustle

down the hall
>thump, creak

in the kitchen
>clang, clink

to the car
>click, slam

on the road
>honk, screech

at the office
>tick, ring

out to lunch
>munch, slurp

return home
>thug, moan

on to bed
>shuffle, snore.

>CATHY CHRISTENSEN, Adult


There are two kinds of onomatopoeia. *Squeal, thump, crunch,* and *squish* are examples of obvious onomatopoeia. When used in moderation, these words enhance and broaden the meaning and sensory impact of a poem. When used in excess, the writing becomes absurd, comic, or exaggerated. The other type of onomatopoeia is subtle and suggested by the shape of the mouth or by the volume of sound when the words are pronounced. Say *round, open, shut, tiny, strike, caress, float,* and *gigantic.* Notice the form of your mouth and volume of your voice when you say them. The sound and shape of these words resemble the actual meanings. Many words contain this more subtle form of onomatopoeia.

Listen to the onomatopoeia in the poems below. Then do the exercise on the pages that follow.

### VIOLA

Music flows like a river
streaming out of my viola.
I listen to the musical waves,
rolling through my viola,
keeping tempo,
like the rhythm of the sea.

JENNY MILLER, age 14


Jumping bronzed walls
over green lakes
where fish go head first
and dolphins lunge
with a swirl,
sea gulls carry faith
for days to come,
leaping higher
to distant peaks.

MATT LANGHANS, age 12

## Activity: Writing with Onomatopoeia

---

**A.** From the list below, select a thing or place that has many sounds.

| | |
|---|---|
| a concert | animals |
| television | a vacation |
| breakfast, lunch, or dinner | a radio |
| a vacuum cleaner | a car, plane, bike, or train |
| firecrackers | a musical instrument |
| a holiday | a test |
| a train | a football game |
| a refrigerator | a hike |
| a typewriter | an office |
| an argument | a restaurant |
| sleep | a city or section of a city |
| a party | your house |

**B.** Write a poem describing the place or thing using the onomatopoeic words on the next page. To hear the effect of onomatopoeia, write more than one poem and vary the number of onomatopoeic words you use in each poem. See Cori's poem on the next page for an example.

## Onomatopoeic Words

| | | |
|---|---|---|
| bang | ding dong | ring |
| beep | drip | rip |
| blink | fizz | roar |
| boom | flip flop | rustle |
| bow wow | grate | sizzle |
| buzz | gurgle | slap |
| chirp | grind | slurp |
| chug | hiss | smack |
| clang | honk | snap |
| clap | hum | splash |
| clatter | lunge | squeak |
| click | meow | squeal |
| clink | moan | squish |
| cluck | moo | swirl |
| crack | munch | thump |
| crackle | murmur | tic toc |
| crash | ping | warble |
| creak | plop | whack |
| crunch | quack | whisper |
| cuckoo | rattle | yawn |

Cori uses onomatopoeia and you can almost hear the gallop of the horses.

### HORSES

Horses are beautiful, fast, and colorful
They gallop—clop, clop,
And their tails fly
With the beat of the wind.

CORI KNIGHT, age 10

# Unit 7—Repetition

Clap your hands and you create rhythm. **Repetition** in poetry works in a similar way. Like each clap, repeated words and phrases provide emphasis and continuity in poems. Listen carefully and repetition, like applause, may even sound like music.

# Repeating a Word or a Phrase

In articles and reports, writers repeat words to emphasize themes and to make transitions from one part of the writing to another. In poetry, intentional repetition, also called **anaphora**, is used for additional reasons. A significant feature of a poem is its sound. A poet, then, will repeat a word or phrase because of the quality of the sound and the impact it has on the content of the poem. Poets also repeat words or phrases to establish rhythms and structure in their poetry.

On the next few pages, you can see and hear the effects of repetition used in different positions in poems.

**SPIRAL STAIRCASE**

Behind my barbed wired eyes,
I see lightning flash,
the design of
my spiral staircase.

Hammers pound,
nails dance,
candles, my work light
as I construct
my spiral staircase.

Staring at the distant star,
fantasies in play,
I dream about
my spiral staircase.

I'm glad to be around
away from the dark cloud
music sounds from
my spiral staircase.

Then comes the night
windows crack,
ladies scream.
Who else lives
my spiral staircase?

Somebody calls to me
but I turn away
to the crumbling of
my spiral staircase.

Birds sing the wind's song.
I throw down the past
and bury
my spiral staircase.

ERIK HALDI, age 15


If I could capture
 a field of mice
 stored carefully in a matchbox
If I could capture
 a strip of moonbeams
 floating on a cloud
If I could capture
 the glint of sunlight
 on breaking waves
If I could capture
 the fine smell of pine needles
 in my nightshirt
I would be the dreamer dreamed.

ELAINE CHILDS-GOWELL, Adult

## NOT TOO LATE

Lately I see another person here.
Of late I see I've changed.
I used to be late a lot,
Slip in quietly, unnoticed.
Am I a johnny-come-lately?
Seems like I just arrived.

A late bloomer bursting into
Heart-shaped flowers, pink,
serene, sweet and still...
Better late than never.
Most of my life I thought
I'd be never.

Lately I see another person here.
I see the glimpse of forever.
I sit in the branches of the human-tree.
Grand women and children love me.
Even men, tribe from the other side,
Love me—a miracle arrived.

Maybe it was my New Year's scheme.
No long list of labors failed, loves lost.
Two words only: more yeses.
Lately I say yes a lot.
Me and Molly Bloom.
Yes Yes Yes.
Lately I can see forever.

                    LINDA NOE, Adult

# Repeating a Preposition

**Prepositions** show relationships between people, places, and things. Because these relationships are *spatial,* pertaining to space or place, and *temporal,* having to do with time, the repetition of a preposition in poetry emphasizes position, place, and time.

About the roots the base of the tree
I wind myself, my spine, my ankles
and twist my neck.
    About the past I remember nothing,
about all that went before me,
wrapped around living wood,
I prefer to molder in the damp.
    About the depths I plumb
there is little to say, my mouth is closed
by the pressure of blinding rootlets,
grateful for the quiet.
    About all this stop and fallow,
this one-way exit round about I lay twisted
and torn comfortable in my unknowing cozy
in the dark contortion of denial
    About which I know nothing.

                    JILL REYNOLDS, Adult

From the time of my parents
I come to know
From country, crickets at night
Scared sleep was sound.
From songs sung by a fire
Shooting sparks in night sky
From old men telling tales
To children's open ears.

KATHRYN CAMPBELL, Adult

## Activity: Using Prepositions in Poetry

First, choose a preposition from the list below. Then, write a poem in which you repeat this preposition throughout it. Write several poems and vary the placement of your preposition in them. Compose at least one poem with the repetition at the beginnings of the lines.

| | | |
|---|---|---|
| about | by | outside |
| above | down | over |
| across | during | past |
| after | for | through |
| among | from | to |
| around | inside | toward |
| at | into | under |
| before | near | until |
| below | of | up |
| beside | off | with |
| besides | on | without |
| between | out | |

Jacquie opens her poem below with an unusual statement: "In my dreams I am an onion." As you continue reading, you see however that this is no ordinary onion. Her onion is made of silver and dances to the owls and stars. By the time Jacquie repeats the opening line in the second stanza, its meaning has changed. Repetition can stress a theme, or it can, as in "Onion," allow you to measure the shifts in your perspective as you read through a poem.

**ONION**

In my dreams I am an onion
silver and shiny,
peeling down silvery layers,
dancing before the stream of a dark forest
naked and bare to the owls and stars
under branches that release showers of droplets.

In my dreams I am an onion,
sliding under doorways
dancing to the moon,
holding amber in my hands.

An onion is a wonderful thing—
It is solid and comes from the earth.
Without it, soups taste plain
and lettuce leaves no mark
upon the palate.

                              JACQUIE WILLETTE, Adult

# Unit 8—Derived Poems

Poets usually start with an emotion, image, or idea, and then use words to develop it. They can, however, begin in the other direction and start with words. Words trigger a variety of pictures, feelings, and memories. Say the words *Thanksgiving, summer vacation,* and *work,* and then notice how different ideas and images emerge from them.

In this chapter, you will write **derived poems**. You will begin with another poet's words and then let the theme of your poem develop from them.

What is the value of using another writer's words? By incorporating these words in your poems, you can expand your word pool. Words suggest themes, so your range of topics may broaden. This exercise taps your intuition, contests writer's block, and encourages you to take risks with your style, topics, and content.

On the next pages, consider the way three poets create derived poems using words from Carl Sandburg's "Sunsets." Notice the differences in the voices, styles, and themes in these poems even though they primarily use the same words.

## Words from "Sunsets" by Carl Sandburg:

| | | |
|---|---|---|
| there | level | stars |
| are | even | ears |
| sunsets | sleep | prairie |
| who | easy | sashes |
| whisper | fling | sea |
| a | scarves | hips |
| good-by | half | rim |
| it | to | dancing |
| is | the | they |
| short | arc | here |
| dusk | over | go |
| way | ribbons | tosses |
| for | at | |
| little | dreams | |

## THE SUNSET

At the dusk of life
When it is time to say good-by,
A sunset appears on the horizon.
When dreams have been tossed
And the heart a dry land,
The muted sky whispers sadness.

When the heart has been light
As ribbons waving in the wind,
Twirling with music
And love
And laughter,
Color dances across the sky
Cheering good-by.
The triumphant song is sung
Hereafter.

BETH ASHLEY, Adult


There are short people
who sleep little dreams
tossing half the sashes
in a fling.

Here, off their hips,
and there, over their ears,
covers in an arc,
fly and dance into a sea
of colorful scarves and ribbons
as pulled from the flappy sleeve
of a mad magician.

DONNA JENNINGS, Adult

In her sleep, dancing came easy,
whether at dusk just beneath the stars
or down by the sea,
where the sunset hung like ribbons in the sky.

She would fling herself in the air
to music only she could hear.
Tossing a scarf over her shoulder
and tightening the sash at her hips,
her feet moved to the rhythm that was in her heart.

It was always hard to say good-bye,
for reality was a chair, shriveled legs, and no dancing.
Good-bye, good-bye, she whispered,
I'll be back again.

SONJA BENNETT, Adult

## Activity: Writing Derived Poems

Choose a poem you like and list the words in it. Make
a running list or group the words by parts of speech.
Then write a poem using the words in the list, adding
your own as needed.

# Unit 9—Inquiry

I had a teacher who used to say that it is as important to make **inquiries** or ask questions as it is to answer them. Questions prepare us to receive information. Poetry writing is an ideal form for asking and answering questions, a way to develop ideas and get new insights.

In "Whisper," Tip asks questions and gives surprising answers.

## WHISPER

I asked the mountain which way to climb.
She turned her white shoulder, shivered, and shook
And out of her shadow she whispered..."You know."

I asked the melon..."How do you know your own seed?"
She smiled and beamed her bloated belly
Bearing weight as she watched my wonderings
and whispered..."You know."

I asked the music..."Why are you sweet?"
She laughed out loud, lanky and loose,
floating over lovers and roofs
And listened to my heart whisper..."You know."

I ask myself..."Why do I ask why?"
And the mountain chuckles and the melon grins
And the music sounds, and they love that I ask
So they can whisper..."You know."

TIP TOLAND, Adult

# Questioning Something in Nature

People are often inspired by nature. Poets extend this connection. When they question nature, they can use the physical and symbolic features of these things in their responses.

## Activity: Ask Nature

First, choose a topic from the list below. Then, on a separate sheet of paper, ask questions and answer them from nature's point of view. On the next page, Mischelly and Judith question the desert, fire, and ice.

### I asked the....

| | | |
|---|---|---|
| moon | mountain | fire |
| stone | air | well |
| stars | desert | breeze |
| sun | ocean | day |
| sky | rainbow | clouds |
| tree | shadow | island |
| wind | earth | tides |
| forest | rain | valley |
| night | rock | coal |
| granite | flower | diamond |
| galaxy | forest | river |

**DESERT**

I asked the desert to welcome me.
It lifted a red, tufted mesa
straight into the cobalt sky.
I asked the desert
to be my friend.
It ran with hot dry winds
across the piñons for days.
I asked the desert
for its secret.
It opened its heart of hearts
to stillness.

                    MISCHELLY DEGROOT, Adult


I asked the fire—Will you burn me?
        Surely not.
I asked the ice—Will you cut me?
        I will glide past.
I asked the bog—Will I sink?
        You may.
I asked the lightning—Why did you miss me?
        It replied, You were sleeping.
                    JUDITH FRANZ, Adult


# Questioning Contents

---

Poets can even question everyday things. When they
ask what is in a computer, for example, they can give
literal answers, such as "wires" and "circuit boards" or
imagined responses, such "hopes" and "ideas."

## Activity: Questioning Contents

On a separate sheet of paper, complete the question, "What's in my...?" using any of the following subjects. Then write a poem answering your question.

| | | | |
|---|---|---|---|
| drawers | head | dreams | computer |
| car | hands | summer | past |
| closet | journal | diary | purse |
| heart | trunk | eyes | glasses |
| laundry | work | clothes | refrigerator |

Al and Ryan, below, and Jill, on the next page, answer their questions with real and imagined responses.

**WHAT'S IN MY GOAT?**

Weird things like soup cans
and a sense of humor,
the postman's shoe,
and grandpa's pipe,
the rare wisdom to be quiet,
and the serenity to be seen.

AL CHASE, Adult

**WHAT'S IN MY HANDS?**

In these hands I hold
vertical shades of gray and silver.
Colors diminish
as my fingers size up hope.

Later, light glows bright
and my hands hold promise
of a sky filled with laughter.

RYAN MACKLE, age 12

## WHAT'S IN MY PENCIL?

Lost civilizations not yet built.
A letter to my dead grandmother that asks,
"Just where are you exactly?"
A tentatively balanced checkbook,
a telephone scribble, my next forgotten appointment.
There is a line a mile long,
ambling down the sidewalk,
depositing graphite on the rough pavement,
shouldering past the dusty chalk
of a hopscotch game,
disappearing under fall leaves
on its way to the post office.
It never makes it.
But dies conveniently in front of the art supply store
where I go in and buy another.

I continue.
There's a shadow to fill in
a monster to illuminate, a baby's face to caress.
Eye-hand coordination is what it's all about,
training the pencil to manifest the twist
and tremble of gesture and pulse.
In my pencil is as much of the universe
as I can funnel through my arm.
Re-member.
Now comes the prayer—
the ebony point takes on a life of its own
as it moves across the paper
like a Ouija Board—Stay sharp.
                    Don't break.
                    Forget the eraser.
                    JILL REYNOLDS, Adult

# Unit 10—Rhyme

Rhyme was the most widely used poetic technique in English poetry from the twelfth century until the middle of the twentieth century. **Rhyme** structures and contains a poem, often moving the reader quickly and easily to the end of a line. Rhyme can hum a melody like a flute or set a rhythm like a drum.

**Rhyme** is often the first thing a reader hears in a poem, but it is only one of the many elements that give shape and breadth to poetry. Rhyme is most effective when used with the other poetic techniques. Notice how William uses detailed description and rhyme in his poem.

### A PLACE, PEACEFUL AND FREE

Out in space, far, far away
Is a place I want to visit someday.
Peaceful and quiet with sun all around
And wild flowers on soft fragrant ground.

Tall trees up high and moss below
With streams and rivers that sparkle and glow.
Radiant lakes, fish of all kinds,
Bright colored birds with songs like chimes.

Flowers with scents that caress my nose,
Small caterpillars that tickle my toes.
Cute, furry creatures all over the place,
Fluffy butterflies that land on my face.

On soft white clouds in blankets of blue,
Dreams and fantasies all come true,
This is a place, peaceful and free.
This is the place where I long to be.

WILLIAM WHITE, age 11

In the following poems, William and Mel use rhyme as well as metaphor, simile, alliteration, imagery, and personification.

## MOUNTAIN HIDEAWAY

Two hawks soar and dive peacefully in the wind.
A bird, like a flute, sings to a child.
The hillside sits as still as a statue
As the great oak watches quietly in the wild.

WILLIAM WHITE, age 11

## APPLE SCRUFFS

George and me, we're old apple scruffs
weathered skins, smooth and tough,
resting on porches, listening to trees,
forest, rivers, and mountain streams.

George says, Go get our bikes.
Apple scruffs just pack and hike
on back roads near misty peaks
where nobody has to speak.

Let us go, he says to me.
We'll take off from the balmy trees
in our hiking suits and moccasins,
green hair blowing in the wind.

MEL CARTER, age 18

# Types of Rhyme

There are two major types of rhyme, exact rhyme and near rhyme. **Exact**, or **pure rhyme**, shown in the poems below, occurs when words have identical final sounds.

### THE COLOR PERIWINKLE

The color periwinkle is shaped like wavy *hair*,
sounds like a small breeze high in the *air*,
feels like a soft airy *cloud*,
and makes me feel like humming softly out *loud*.
It looks like a reflection of the clearest sunny *day*,
is the month of *May*,
is the song of a *dove*,
is a box of sky fragments from *above*.

PETER KIRKPATRICK, age 10

### HAIKU

With my dog as my *guide*
I travel a long journey
On our *mountainside*.

GERRY OLSON, Adult

### FOOTBALL

The crowd was *tense*.
The team was on *defense*.
The pass was *good*.
Everyone *stood*.
Oh boy, what *suspense*!

FRED MILES, age 11

**Near rhyme**, also called **off** or **inexact rhyme**, occurs between words with similar, although not identical, sounds. Poets create near rhyme by using assonance, consonance, and alliteration in their poems.

Delphine's and Lainie's poems use **assonance**, the repetition of the same vowel sound.

Robustly treading, I will s<u>ee</u>.
Deeply br<u>ea</u>thing, I will know.
Always b<u>ei</u>ng, I will wonder.
Ever-r<u>ea</u>ching, I will meld
Warrior with a b<u>e</u>ginner's mind.
DELPHINE BOWERS, Adult

### CAMPFIRE CIRCLE

A c<u>oo</u>l m<u>oo</u>n gazes on.
Tiny twigs sm<u>o</u>ke and catch,
crackling warmth into the circle
of surrounding st<u>o</u>ne.
LAINIE RILEY, Adult

**Consonance** is repetition of the same consonant sounds in words with different main vowels. It also creates near rhyme, especially when the consonance occurs at the ends of words, as in *little* and *rattle* or *mice* and *space*. The inexact rhyme in Susan's poem below contributes to its humor.

### POETRY CLASS

All week long we've thought and though<u>t</u>
And many answers we have go<u>t</u>.
Alliteration, I'm sorry to say, happens to the dropout.

Synesthesia? What the doctor gives just so you won't pout.
Triplets always lead to trouble as three we know's a crowd.
Symbol is, of course, an instrument quite loud.
Onomatopoeia is a swamp, I'm almost sure.
And pronouns, quite simply, are no longer amateur.
Assonance, don't ask me, any 9th grade boy can say.
Metaphor, the best of all, means we met yesterday.
Simile is two brothers, Sim and his twin, Lee.
And coordinating conjunction? A couple kissing, finally.
SUSAN BEAUCHAMP, Adult

**Eye rhyme** or **visual rhyme** occurs when two or more words *look* like they rhyme rather than *sound* like they rhyme. Eye rhyme, shown below, is a type of end or terminal alliteration.

And there upon her jewel crowned *head*
She wore King Rupert's silver *bead.*
BARBARA JACKSON, Adult

You can climb the *root,*
*Foot* following *foot* in the dim air.
BARBARA TURNER, Adult

# End Rhyme

Rhyme that occurs at the ends of lines of poetry is called **end rhyme**. End rhyme is the element people most frequently associate with poetry. This type of rhyme is particularly challenging to write and one of the reasons why many people believe they can never write poems. The popularization of free verse, however, frees poets from the myth that all poems must rhyme. Now writers can use rhyme to strengthen the content, not because it is the only available poetic form.

## Guidelines for Writing with End Rhyme

**1.** *Use rhyme to enhance the meaning of your poem.* When two words rhyme, neither word must sound secondary or incidental. When I first started teaching poetry, a boy in my class wrote "I have a car. It is pink. In it is a kitchen sink." While the image of a pink car seemed plausible and even poetic, the absurdity of the kitchen sink indicated that the writer got stuck for a rhyming word and randomly chose one. When you write poems that rhyme, *use only rhyming words that fit the content.*

**2.** *Consider memorizing poems that rhyme to become familiar with the way that rhyme structures poetry.* I heard a story on the radio that illustrates the power of rhyme. Two men with little experience decided to climb a mountain in India. About four hours from the summit, they realized they did not have the endurance to make it to the top and thought they might die on the mountain. To stay awake, they decided to recite poems they had memorized forty years before. They credited the poetry with bolstering their stamina and giving them rhythm to reach the top.

Memorization will support your writing, freeing you to recall sounds and rhythms without the printed page. Memorize a favorite poem. Rhymed poetry is like a good friend, ready to climb that mountain with you.

## Determining the Rhyme Pattern

To determine the rhyme scheme in a poem with end rhyme, assign each line a letter of the alphabet. Lines with last words that rhyme are given the same letter.

### EAGLE

| | |
|---|---|
| Clouds float free upon the sky, | *a* |
| But everything's still when an eagle dies. | *a* |
| It's graceful and quick with lightning speed | *b* |
| And snags a fish without being seen. | *b* |
| But people shoot eagles just like they're game. | *c* |
| It's like shooting a son—it only brings pain. | *c* |

FRED MILES, age 11

| | |
|---|---|
| The sun danced | *a* |
| across the sky. | *b* |
| The rainbow curved | *a* |
| for miles high. | *b* |
| Where does the rainbow end? | *c* |

DAVE MICHAELS, age 14

### HIGHWAY

| | |
|---|---|
| Wheels swim across the wavy highway | *a* |
| waiting to reach the beach. | *b* |
| It seems to go on forever, | *c* |
| so far out of reach. | *b* |
| All alone, no one to talk with or see. | *d* |
| The highway is an ocean, | *e* |
| no life at all but me. | *d* |

ERIK HALDI, age 15

# Unique Rhyme Schemes

Poets create **unique rhyme schemes** or follow set structures called **fixed forms**. Jason's poems, below and on the next page, show how a unique rhyming pattern can support an unexpected shift in the action or help create a wistful mood.

### EARLY DAWN

| | |
|---|---|
| Winter snow, | *a* |
| it feels like thirty below. | *a* |
| Outside, | *b* |
| and I see a light glow | *a* |
| —could be a fawn— | *c* |
| off in the distance | *d* |
| of early dawn. | *c* |

JASON WILLITS, age 11

Out there where the Eskimos live,        *a*
it's a hundred below zero.        *b*
Out in igloos eating homemade stew;        *c*
then the fishing boats come in view.        *c*
They've caught a whale,        *d*
now the hunt is through.        *c*
No more trudging        *e*
across the tundra.        *f*

JASON WILLITS, age 11

# Fixed Rhyme Patterns

There are a variety of fixed or traditional poetic forms. A **stanza** is a group of lines similar in appearance to a paragraph. **Couplets**, **triplets**, and **quatrains** are types of stanzas that give poems a fixed structure. A **limerick** is a traditional structure with a rhyme pattern of *a a b b a*.

A **couplet** is two lines of poetry. Couplets often rhyme, as in Caitlin's poem below. Couplets are generally written in uninterrupted passages. The poem on the next page, "Fishing," has eight couplets.

Halloween is very keen
On Halloween you're never lean.

CAITLIN McELROY, age 9

**FISHING**

I like to go out with my dad on a boat.
And fish and wear the sun for a coat.
We drop our nets or fishing pole line
And everything turns out just fine.
We wait with our poles so patiently
And hope to catch a fish or three.
Then it gets as dark as night.
My dad shows me all the lights
Especially the one far out in space.
Dad calls it the moon, a very strange place.
Dad talks of pirates who guided ships
By stars on long and lonely trips.
He tells of monsters in the sea
That swallow ships and frightens me.
When our trip is over and waves turn to foam,
We pack up our gear and head towards our home.

BILL MUSSELMAN, age 12

A **triplet** is a group of three lines. In the poems below
and on the next page, Jacquie and Caitlin wrote triplets
(in rhyme using an *a a a* rhyme scheme).

| | |
|---|---|
| Spring creeps slowly down the *moor* | *a* |
| And leaves its footprints near my *door* | *a* |
| As sunlight tails across the *floor.* | *a* |
| | |
| In my yard the tulips *rise* | *b* |
| Trumpets in a floral *guise.* | *b* |
| My heart has grown one year *wise.* | *b* |

JACQUIE WILLETTE, Adult

Scares are full of *dares*.                 *a*
Scares pop up your *hairs*.                  *a*
Scares bring lots of *stares*.               *a*

                    CAITLIN McELROY, age 9

A **quatrain** is a four line stanza, and, when rhymed, assumes a variety of patterns. Familiar rhyme schemes are *a b b a, a a b b,* and *a b a b,* but the most common quatrain pattern is *a b c b.*

**SPHERE**

The waves turn round in arches,              *a*
curve downward and greet the *shore*.        *b*
The sun's a ball of fire,                    *c*
telling of gods and old *folklore*.          *b*

The moon is a scoop of ice cream
in a chocolate covered *sky*,
and a star's a ball of fire
whose points won't be *denied*.

And we stand here in a circle
with friends clasped hand to *hand*
as we start our circle procession
all across this *land*.

Our goal is to breathe in this circle
and turn it into a *sphere*
and learning the lessons of nature.
put depth in place of *fear*.

                    MYRA ECKSTEIN, age 17

# Writing a Limerick

A **limerick** is a poetic form for writing humor. Limericks have five lines written in the rhyme scheme *a a b b a*. Limericks were traditionally written in meter, but meter is now often replaced by line length. The poems below show limericks without meter. Write a limerick in which lines one, two, and five are long, and lines three and four are short (*a a b b a*).

**JOHN**

| | |
|---|---|
| I once knew a man named John. | *a* |
| He loved to fish in Black Pond. | *a* |
| But it dried up. | *b* |
| What bad luck. | *b* |
| Now the fish can't spawn. | *a* |

**LEE**

There once was a fish named Lee
Who loved to swim and roam free
He laughed and joked
Till he almost choked
Now his label is Chicken of the Sea.

**GORE**

I had a good friend named Gore
Who used to love to hunt boar.
But the boar he found
Chased him around.
Now Gore doesn't hunt boar any more.

BILL MUSSELMAN, age 12

## Activity: Writing with End Rhyme

There is a particular challenge and reward to writing with rhyme. You not only attend to the content of the poem, but you empower and shape it through the use of sounds.

Write a poem in which the lines end in rhyme. You may want to use one of the topics listed below.

### Choose a topic:

| | |
|---|---|
| the weather | a place |
| a season | your family |
| a month | an animal |
| a holiday | a trip |
| a car | |

### Activity Ideas

**1.** Write a poem with a unique rhyming pattern.

**2.** Write a couplet, a triplet, and a quatrain using the same topic.

**3.** Expand a couplet, a triplet, or a quatrain into a longer poem.

**4.** Write a limerick (see page 101 for the form).

**5.** Rewrite a magazine or newspaper article as a poem with end rhyme.

**6.** Write five to ten "I Am" metaphors (see pages 13 and 14). Then use them in a poem that rhymes.

# Internal Rhyme

There are two main types of **internal rhyme**, or rhyme within lines of poetry. One type rhymes words in the middle of lines with words at the ends of the lines (see Andy's poem below). The second poem, by Dave, uses the other type of internal rhyme which rhymes words within lines with other words in the middle of lines of the poem.

Waves roll across the sand.
As a sea gull flies overhead,
the sun seems to beat down on the water
like a magnifying glass.
Cool breeze carries the smell of salt
and clean air.
Rain makes the *land* misty.
Waves smash across the *sand*
as a killer whale swims by.

ANDY BOLLES, age 17

He always *dreams* of snow in December,
but when the sun *gleams* seventy degrees,
he knows a surfboard's better than a sled.

DAVE MICHAELS, age 14

## Activity: Writing in Rhyme

**1.** Choose a poem written in rhyme and rewrite it in free verse.

**2.** Choose a topic. Write it as free verse and then in rhyme in each of these forms: couplet, triplet, and quatrain.

**3.** Write a poem with end rhyme. Then edit it so the rhyme falls within, rather than at the ends, of the lines.

**4.** Write a poem combining free verse and rhyme.

**5.** Use your writing from the alliteration worksheet on pages 64 and 65.

**6.** Choose a serious topic and write about it in rhyme. What are the strengths or weaknesses of composing your topic in rhyme?

**7.** Are you able to effectively cover all themes in rhyme, or do you prefer to use rhyme with certain topics only?

# Unit 11—Meter

There are rhythms in everything we do. Our breathing and the beating of our hearts occur in patterns. Traffic and machinery have distinct rhythms. We see cycles in the weather, the planets, and the seasons. Speech has rhythms of dialect and inflection. Poetry written in **meter** also occurs in patterns that we can measure and hear.

For more than four hundred years, from Shakespeare's time to the middle of this century, English poetry was predominantly written in **meter**—that is, regular patterns of heavily and lightly stressed syllables. The heavily stressed syllables in a poem are referred to as **accented**, and the lightly stressed syllables are called **unaccented**.

The basic metrical unit or pattern is called a **foot**. The iamb, trochee, anapest, dactyl, and spondee are the most commonly used feet. Notice the regular, or measurable, rhythm in Joy's poem.

### ON DECK

Mists rest on the ocean
breezes kiss the deck
Lightly sways the masthead
Ocean's rolling trek

Held gently in your arms
I call your vastness home
and leave the earth behind
For waters where I roam

To watch the humpback whales
Breeching surface seas
Dancing with the puffins—
Nature's panoply

                JOY GREENBERG, Adult

# Metrical Patterns

An **iamb** or **iambic foot** is the standard metrical unit because it relates so closely to the rhythms of walking, breathing, talking, and the beating of the heart. An iamb is an unaccented syllable followed by an accented syllable ( ˘da ´DA ).

˘the ´girl
to ˘love ´
˘arrange ´
amaze

A **trochee** or **trochaic foot** is the reverse of the iamb, but it also has the rhythm of talking, walking, and breathing. A trochee is an accented syllable followed by an unaccented syllable ( ´DA ˘da ).

´lover ˘
´strike ˘it
´water ˘

An **anapest** or **anapestic foot** is made up of two unaccented syllables followed by one accented syllable ( ˘da ˘da ´DA ).

˘ ˘ ´intercede
˘or ˘the ´house
˘as ˘a ´bird
˘with ˘her ´love

A **dactyl** or **dactylic foot** is the reverse of an anapest. A dactyl is one accented syllable followed by two unaccented syllables ( DÁ d̆a d̆a ).

carelessly
marry them
syllable
Julliet

A **spondee** or **spondaic foot** is two stressed syllables ( DÁ DÁ ).

greenhouse
stronghold
run, dance
safeguard

## Activity: Metrical Feet

Using the space on this page and the next, classify the following words according to type of metrical foot. Use a dictionary and look up the accents in the pronunciation, if necessary.

**Example:** **Spondee (spondaic foot)** *DA DA*
        **horseshoe**

1. continent
2. happy
3. misty
4. broken
5. prepared
6. angrily
7. someone
8. flexible
9. consonant
10. concerned
11. interview
12. pavements
13. lyrical
14. madrigal
15. usually
16. wander
17. memory
18. merchant
19. rely
20. water
21. purchase
22. grievance
23. memory
24. destitute
25. purchase
26. compute
27. money
28. market
29. restlessly
30. repair

**Iamb (iambic foot)** *da DA*

_____

_____

_____

_____

_____

**Trochee (trochaic foot)** *DA da*

_____

_____

_____

_____

_____

**Anapest (anapestic foot)** *da da DA*

_____

_____

_____

_____

_____

**Dactyl (dactylic foot)** *DA da da*

_____

_____

_____

_____

_____

**Spondee (spondaic foot)** *DA DA*

_____

_____

_____

_____

_____

# Determining the Metrical Pattern

**Scansion** is the process of marking the metrical pattern of a poem. When you "scan" a poem, you label the stressed syllables with accents ( ͜ ) and the unstressed syllables with the symbol ( ∪ ). The stress that words and syllables receive is not completely fixed but is influenced by the placement of words within the poem and the way the poem is read.

### AMAR

Amar, the gilded bird is dead,
And on his pillow he does leave
Perfumed feathers from his head,
The shadow of his love does grieve.
He sings not in the patterned night,
And all the silent ways of dawn
Are empty of his crested flight.

JACQUIE WILLETTE, Adult

The study of meter includes the *type of foot* (iambic, trochaic, anapestic, dactylic, spondaic) and the *number of feet per line* : A **foot** is the basic measured unit in a poem. It can be iambic ( ∪ ͜ ), trochaic ( ͜ ∪ ), anapestic ( ∪ ∪ ͜ ), or any other type of metrical pattern. Lines of poetry are called different names depending on how many feet are in them.

| Feet per line | Line name |
|---|---|
| one | monometer |
| two | dimeter |
| three | trimeter |

| Feet per line | Line name |
| --- | --- |
| four | tetrameter |
| five | pentameter |
| six | hexameter |
| seven | heptameter |
| eight | octameter |

Barbara's poem, "Support," is written in iambic meter. Each line is a monometer. The rhythm *da DA* occurs one time per line. Monometer is rarely used because it departs from the rhythm and structure of normal speech.

**SUPPORT**

And I
will cry
if you
go too.
But prove
your move
is good
and could
advance
your stance,
then I
will sigh,
but still
I will
kiss you
a fond
adieu.

BARBARA JACKSON, Adult

Iambic tetrameter and trochaic pentameter are shown below. These poetic lines conform to regular patterns of English speech and provide the writer with enough space on each line for a subject, verb, and object. Raina wrote "Wedding Night" in iambic tetrameter; the metrical pattern *da DA* occurs four times per line.

**WEDDING NIGHT**

I join with you, my love, my wife
Our hearts as vast as blanket sands
That know the tides and weather strife
As partners firm cross ocean's hands.

And I will rise a house new borned
That welcomes you come home each day
With roses, daisies, all adorned,
In fragrance of my love's bouquet.

RAINA TOKAR, Adult

We can hear the drum beat throughout A. J.'s poem below, "Mom." It is written in trochaic tetrameter; the rhythm *DA da* occurs four times per line.

**MOM**

Now's the time for me to leave you
Make my way and meet my trials
Learn and live and dance and cry some.
Do not wait for me this while.

Know, dear mom, I really love you.
Thank you greatly for your giving.
I am eighteen, need to leave, so
Turn your love into forgiving.

Bless me nightly, hold me closer
Than you ever have before.
Trust your teachings all these years; your
Wisdom's here, in my heart's core.

A. J. JORDAN, age 17

Poets generally choose a predominant meter and vary it with other patterns so their poems do not become boring and predictable. Used in combination with other meters, the anapest is still characterized by a sing-song quality. One of my classes wrote "Camping" to illustrate anapestic dimeter (the rhythm *da da DA* occurs two times per line).

### CAMPING

In the night near the shore
The boats rest for new lore.
Six young paddlers all ears
Now relinquish their fears.

And the coals soon burn down.
So they dream in sleep's crown.
Of fine birds and six whales
Dreaming their fairy tales.

The dactylic foot establishes a heavy rhythm. Notice how the light content of Raina's poem is weighted by the pattern *DA da da*, which occurs three times per line.

Go softly, night beckons, round the stars.
Dance in there, fielding the magical.
Seasons are singing that love is ours.
                    RAINA TOKAR, Adult

**Blank verse** is often written as unrhymed iambic pentameter. Blank verse gives writing a structure and rhythm without the restrictions of rhyme. It approximates speech more closely than rhymed iambic pentameter.

### HANNIBAL

So Hannibal then took an oath when he
Was young declaring his fidelity
To Africa, and Rome was villainized
And target to thirty-five years of his wars.
He lead his elephants over the hills.
And struck considerable fear and hate
Among his foes. He rode the Pyrenees.
In honor and in arrogance and with
Belief that God would favor the victors.
                    BARBARA JACKSON, Adult

# Haiku

Like blank verse, **haiku** is poetry written in unrhymed meter. In English, meter means the pattern of stressed and unstressed syllables in a poem while in haiku, meter is the count of syllables per line. The meter or measurement of haiku is three lines of 5-7-5 syllables per line.

| | |
|---|---|
| Sixty-five years old! | **5** |
| The body fails, but the world | **7** |
| Still felt with Child's Heart. | **5** |

GERRY OLSON, Adult

Brown-yellow wheatfield
Biggest beautiful plain
Never ending to me.

PETER KIRKPATRICK, age 10

Love is joy
Like roses in a garden
Yours to give away.

WENDY SMITH, age 15

Because haiku is a Japanese form, standard English often does not easily fit into this structure. The vast differences in the English and Japanese languages often require poets to waive strict adherence to the 5-7-5 syllabication of traditional haiku. In English, then, haiku often refers to a three line poem that honors the traditional Japanese themes of nature, change, and insight.

# Writing a Sonnet

A **sonnet** gives you the opportunity to use all your poetic skills in one form. This traditional structure specifies meter, line length, and rhyme scheme. For more than four hundred years, it was the most widely used form in English poetry.

The Shakespearean or English sonnet has fourteen lines in rhymed iambic pentameter. These lines are grouped in three quatrains (groups of four lines) with rhyme schemes of *a b a b, c d c d,* and *e f e f,* followed by a couplet, *g g,* which summarizes the sonnet or ends it with a bold comment. Barbara's poem, below, makes an eloquent statement about the value of writing a sonnet.

### SONNET

| | |
|---|---|
| When I sit down to write a poem, my head | *a* |
| Goes numb and all the thoughts I had are gone, | *b* |
| As puckered as a puff-ball, and as dead— | *a* |
| Grey dust, where once a round white toadstool shone. | *b* |
| A puff-ball trodden by a hobnail boot | *c* |
| Is no more empty than my head feels now | *d* |
| No flatter, no less severed from the root; | *c* |
| My thoughts, the spores that scattered anyhow. | *d* |
| Is it too much to hope that on some lawn | *e* |
| Not far from here, by processes profound | *f* |
| In darkened circles where the grass has gone | *e* |
| The fairy rings are dancing on the ground? | *f* |
| Perhaps they also serve who sit and dream | *g* |
| Of darkness and a place where toadstools gleam. | *g* |

BARBARA TURNER, Adult

## Activity Ideas: Writing in Meter

**1.** Write five lines of poetry, one in each of the following: iambic monometer, iambic dimeter, iambic trimeter, iambic tetrameter, and iambic pentameter.

**2.** Write a metaphor. Rewrite it in each of the following metrical feet: iambic, trochaic, anapestic, dactylic, and spondaic.

**3.** Write one line of poetry in each of the following metrical patterns: iambic, trochaic, anapestic, dactylic, and spondaic.

**4.** Select a poem written in free verse and rewrite it in meter or choose a poem with a dominant meter and vary it.

**5.** Write a poem in meter.

**6.** Write a speech or a historical narrative in blank verse, unrhymed iambic pentameter.

**7.** Write a short poem in free verse. Rewrite it in blank verse, unrhymed iambic pentameter. Write a third draft in iambic pentameter, rhymed verse.

**8.** Write a sonnet (see the previous page for the form).

# Unit 12—Tone

We can often tell how someone feels by listening to the tone of his or her voice. Like a person's voice, a poem also has a **tone** or mood that shows a feeling or an attitude that the poet wants to convey. The poem may seem sad, happy, funny, sarcastic, angry, or carefree, and the words, themes, and structures of the poem contribute to this tone.

One way to create **tone** is through choice of words. When a poem begins with an article ( *a, the* ), an adjective ( *green, famous* ), or a noun ( *eagle, summer* ), the initial focus is on a *thing*. By starting a poem with a preposition, an adverb, or a conjunction, you affect the mood of your poem by putting the focus on *time, possibility,* and *place.* Ryan establishes tone in his poem "Jungle" by starting it with the word *if.*

**JUNGLE**

If I could capture life in a jungle,
I would feel safe now.
Instead I'm waiting
for the artificial horizon to set
beneath the fixed position clouds.

The jungle laughs
as I try to make life-extending decisions
knowing their life-ending mistakes.

Planes circle overhead
like falcons waiting for prey.
Is this a dream,
or an unsynchronized, anesthetic nightmare?

Wrong times and wrong places
lengthen the war memorial.
                    RYAN MACKLE, age 12

## Activity: Creating a Tone

On a separate sheet of paper, write a poem that begins
with a preposition, an adverb, or a conjunction to
create a tone or mood that emphasizes time, space, or
possibility.

| Prepositions | Adverbs | Conjunctions |
|---|---|---|
| about | carefully | after |
| above | closely | after all |
| after | finally | because |
| at first | lately | before |
| before | nearly | however |
| below | recently | if |
| behind | silently | unless |
| between | slowly | until |
| in | so | when |
| outside | softly | whenever |
| toward | soon | where |
| to | suddenly | while |
| under | too | |
| with | | |
| without | | |

## Activity: Creating Tone Through Place

Rachel begins her poem, shown below, with the words "In my dreams I am in...." The reference to a dream allows her to put herself in an improbable place, the inside of a syrup bottle. Consider preceding your opening preposition, adverb, or conjunction with one of the following phrases to establish a tone or mood that stresses feelings, goals, or dreams.

In my wishes, I am...    In my past, I was...

In my dreams, I am...    In my stories, I was...

In my fears, I am...    In the future, I'll be...

In my nightmares, I am...

### SAP

In my dreams,
I am in Mrs. Butterworth's oblong bottle,
slow procrastinating syrup
hiding inside this trusted woman.
How many maples were drained
of their sweetness to create me?
I am manufactured by owners.
I am crouched down low
behind her wide apron,
feeling thick and sluggish,
thinking...
and watching others on the outside
eating their pancakes and eggs
while I am continuously tipped over.
Can't break through her stomach yet.

Mrs. Butterworth's not ready
to let me be free.
Confused...
Am I supposed to enjoy
the sugar sweetness
or is it just tree sap?

                RACHEL McLEOD, age 17

# Absurdity

After the armadillo
finished giving his speech
on sub-nuclear physics,
the cow realized it was his turn.

                RYAN MACKLE, age 12

**Absurdity**, or writing in a tone that is silly and contrary to reason, adds humor to poetry and is fun to compose. One effective way to create absurdity is to write about situations in which animals assume human roles.

## Activity: Writing Absurdity

First, name activities such as playing baseball, cooking dinner, driving a car, watching television, doing homework, or reading the newspaper. Then, as in the poems on the next page, create absurdity by describing the events using animals as the main characters, rather than people.

The gorilla and orangutan
were bridge partners,
when the gorilla bid hearts
instead of spades.

The turtle and crab,
the opponents,
laughed,
but they did so softly
because they respected
the etiquette of the game.

CHICKIE KITCHMAN, Adult


Masses of street ducks
robbed the banks.

RYAN MACKLE, age 12


In my bathtub,
my rubber duck planned sabotage.

SHEA JUDD-HUME, age 11


# Parody

A **parody** is a comic or exaggerated imitation of a
work of art, creating a tone of humor in poems. A
parody is most effective when both the writer and
reader are familiar with the original work. The parody
uses key words, phrases, structures, rhymes, themes, or
meter from the original. This allows the poet to suggest
the original without directly referring to it.

## THE ROAD NOT TAKEN

Two roads diverged in a yellow wood,
And sorry I could not travel both
And be one traveler, long I stood
And looked down one as far as I could
To where it bent in the undergrowth;

Then took the other, as just as fair,
And having perhaps the better claim,
Because it was grassy and wanted wear;
Though as for that, the passing there
Had worn them really about the same.

And both that morning equally lay
In leaves no step had trodden black.
Oh, I kept the first for another day!
Yet knowing how way leads on to way,
I doubted if I should ever come back.

I shall be telling this with a sigh
Somewhere ages and ages hence:
Two roads diverged in a wood, and I—
I took the one less traveled by,
And that has made all the difference.

ROBERT FROST, 1874–1963

Al Bandstra read Robert Frost's "The Road Not Taken," above, and wrote a parody of it, shown on the next page. To evoke Frost's poem without specifically referring to it, Al began the first four lines of his poem with the same words Frost used. Al included many other key words, such as *traveler, undergrowth,* and *difference* in his parody. Al also played on Frost's theme, changing choice of life's path into choice of buses.

## THE METRO NOT TAKEN

Two roads converged at the yellow sign
And sorry I do not the Metro know
And be a punctual traveler, there I stood
And looked down the street as far as I could
To see the number 26
disappear in the undergrowth.

So I waited for the other just as fair
And having perhaps the better route
Since it went to 84th
And I was wanted there at 7:00.

I am telling this with a sigh,
Miles and miles of walking since,
I waited for the one that didn't come by
And that made a lot of difference.

AL BANDSTRA, Adult

## Activity: Writing Parody

Choose a poem to parody. Read it a few times to
become familiar with its content and structure. Then list
the key words, themes, and rhymes and use them to
write your own parody.

# Unit 13—Synesthesia

The cooking class in the next room was baking cakes. "Taste that smell," wrote Barbara Jackson. We knew what she meant because the smell was so strong it seemed as though we could taste it. Another person wrote a similar line, "I can touch their hunger." Both sentences are examples of **synesthesia**, the description of one sensory perception by another. Synesthesia is challenging to write at first because we cannot use logic to explain it. Rather, we have to sense its meaning.

**Synesthesia** is an intuitive connecting of the senses, in which one sense is used to describe another. Something not associated with a taste, for example, is described by it, as in *the taste of green*. When you read *the taste of...*, you probably expect something that has a taste to follow, such as hot apple pie, not the word *green*.

Synesthesia works when you suspend logic and engage your intuition; this allows you to sense or imagine words and images not printed on the page, as in *the taste of green* (apple pie) or (he hungered for) *the taste of green* (money).

**MARRIAGE**

We soften the lemonade
with white cotton cloths,
the clear fragrance of a summer evening,
and the warmth from *the sound*
*of our children smiling.*

VICKY EDMONDS VERVER, Adult

*Yellow sounds* like rain on the windows.

CAITLIN McELROY, age 9

Susie *felt the taste* of love
in her grandma's gingerbread hug.

DONNA JENNINGS, Adult

*Look beyond the echo.*

RHEA PEAKE, Adult

## Activity: Writing Synesthesia

For each color or texture listed below, name something *not* associated with a color or a texture.

**Examples**:   *Red* wind
*White* memories
*Smooth* love

**1.** blue _____

**2.** orange _____

**3.** red _____

**4.** velvet _____

**5.** satin _____

**6.** turquoise _____

**7.** opaque _____

**8.** transparent _____

**9.** textured _____

**10.** rough _____

Use the words listed below to write a sentence using things not associated with smell.

**Example**:  I see the six *fragrances* of the sky.

**11.** smell _____

**12.** aroma _____

**13.** bouquet _____

**14.** fragrance/fragrant _____

For the following words, name things not connected with sound.

**Example**: *Hear* the heat.

**15.** listen _____

**16.** hear _____

**17.** beckoning _____

**18.** calling _____

Use the words listed with things not seen.

**Example**: I *looked* into the sound of morning.

**19.** look _____

**20.** see _____

**21.** visualize _____

**22.** picture _____

**23.** gaze _____

Next to the words below, name things you cannot literally touch.

**Example**: *Embrace* the shadow.

**24.** feel _____

**25.** grab _____

**26.** embrace _____

**27.** caress _____

**28.** touch _____

Synesthesia connects the senses. In the following poems, what initially appears illogical begins to seem possible.


I hear the wind
washing my hair with icy fingers
clearing away the weight of the day
and *rinsing it in the moonlight.*
                    VICKY EDMONDS VERVER, Adult


A rustling tree gets my attention
as the wind cools me
from the intelligent sun.
I *smell the crackling* of colored flowers
with the scent of an afternoon frost.

And for some reason I imagine
the whole world looks
like this distant path
unfolding in my mind.
                    VINCE FREEMAN, age 13


There is fragrance in my heart.
I *hear its textures.*
They are both rough and smooth.
I *taste its colors*
They are rainbow-hued.
                    LINDA SHELTON, Adult

# Unit 14—Symbol

The most powerful symbols are things
that occur in nature. When an artist draws
a picture of the sun, it usually symbolizes
or stands for happiness because it reminds
us of light and warmth. Artists probably
would not use the sun to show something
unhappy. In poetry, as in art, the natural
association we have with a **symbol**
greatly influences the way we write and
interpret it.

A **symbol** is a movement, image, word, or sound that represents or stands for a thing, quality, or idea. A symbol is similar to a metaphor and simile. The symbol, however, *implies* a connection between things while the metaphor and simile *state* it. In the poem below, the crows symbolize different things, depending on the reader's point of view.

### CROWS' FEET

The crows come at night
to dance their hard rhythms
around my eyes.

Even as a girl, they swooped
and cawed through those towering oaks
making plans for their nightly visits,
laughing at time.

In the morning, unamused,
my father showered rounds
of empty rifle shots into the leaves,
"just to scare them,"
praying they'd stop.

But they cackle, soaring higher,
wiser, for they understand their job well,
and come again with each night's music
mocking our foolish attempts to keep time still.

      TIP TOLAND, Adult

In poetry there are at least two general types of symbols: universal and personal. A **universal symbol** has a primary or main meaning that is recognized at different times in history and across different cultures. Coined money is a universal symbol of exchange.

A **personal symbol** has significance to particular individuals and groups and assumes different meanings. Water may symbolize refreshment, cleansing, healing, religious ceremony, or commerce, depending on its context.

Symbols are an integral part of our lives, often holding opposite meanings for different groups of people. Cigarettes, for example, might symbolize relief, acceptance, ignorance, and death, depending on one's point of view. Consider the different opinions people hold about the flag, welfare, war, and music.

Symbols are so powerful that people are willing to fight and even die for them. Symbols gather their power, in part, because they assume, rather than state, the connection between two things, blurring the distinction between the object being symbolized and the symbol itself. In the 1960s, for example, men with long hair were sometimes treated rudely. People made assumptions about what their long hair meant, and their hair, in turn, came to stand for a particular set of values and beliefs. Long hair assumed qualities considerably broader than itself. It became a symbol.

Many symbols gather their power through their connection with nature. The sun, earth, and moon are in themselves powerful, and, when used as symbols, they are strengthened from association with the actual objects.

## Activity: Symbols

In the space below, write what each thing or person symbolizes to you, your family, or your community. Compare your answers with those of others. Notice how the same thing or person may assume different, and sometimes contradictory, meanings.

**1.** eagle

---

**2.** tree

---

**3.** ocean

---

**4.** ring

---

**5.** money

---

**6.** flowers

---

**7.** food

---

**8.** telephone

---

**9.** death

---

**10.** letter

---

**11.** Christmas

_____

**12.** birthday

_____

**13.** vacation

_____

**14.** job

_____

**15.** earth

_____

**16.** sun

_____

**17.** moon

_____

**18.** crystals

_____

**19.** dreams

_____

**20.** babies

_____

## Activity: Writing with Symbols

Complete any of the following activity suggestions to practice writing with symbols.

**1.** Write a poem containing a symbol. Use the worksheets on pages 135 and 136 to write a list of what the symbol represents. Then incorporate these words and ideas in your poem.

**2.** Make a list of personal and universal symbols that are important in your life, and tell what they symbolize.

**3.** Tell a story, in poetic form, in which a symbol plays a key part.

**4.** Describe someone or something that serves as a symbol, and then, toward the end of the poem, draw a conclusion or moral.

**5.** Write a poem in which one symbol transforms into another.

**6.** Write about a thing or person that serves as a symbol and then change the meaning of the symbol.

**7.** Start a poem by asking a question about a symbol, and then answer your question.

In her poem "Root," Barbara uses symbols from nature: a root, the earth, and their forest skins.

## ROOT

There is a root.
A nest of earth-clotted limbs
Sheathed in their tough forest skin,
Up-ended in the dim air
Like the snakes of Pompeii
Surprised—terrified—then still forever,
Just where they thought they were safe.

You can climb the root,
Foot following foot in the dim air
Arm through twisted arm
Knee over elbow
Until at last you can shout,
"I'm the king of the castle,"
Down on the dark heads
Of your mother, father, sister.
You can call them what you like.
It doesn't matter.
They won't look up anyway.

Or you can hold the root inside you,
Twisting words and fears together
Between your ribs in a fierce knot,
Lithe as snakes, tough as leather,
Hard as bone.
That way, whenever the time feels right,
You can start to climb.

                    BARBARA TURNER, Adult

# Glossary

**Absurdity**  Writing that is silly or ridiculous and contrary to reason.

**Adjective**  A word that qualifies, defines, or limits a noun or a pronoun.

**Alliteration**  The same, beginning consonant sound in two or more words close together.

**Assonance**  The same vowel sound in two or more words close together.

**Consonance**  The same consonant sound in words close together. The repeating consonant sounds may occur anywhere within the words.

**Derived poems**  Using words from other poems.

**Edit**  Alter to make more suitable; prepare for publication.

**Foot**  Basic metrical unit; the most common feet are the iambic, trochaic, anapestic, dactylic, and spondaic.

**Free verse**  Poetry without end rhyme, set structures, or meter (regular patterns of stressed and unstressed syllables).

**Haiku**  A traditional Japanese form of poetry consisting of three lines with 5-7-5 syllables per line.

**Imagery**  A mental picture.

**Limerick**  A traditional humorous form consisting of five lines. Lines one, two, and five are long and rhyme; lines three and four are short and rhyme.

**Metaphor**  The comparison between two unrelated nouns.

**Meter** Regular patterns of heavily and lightly stressed syllables. An **accented syllable** is a heavily stressed syllable in a poem written in meter. An **unaccented syllable** is a lightly stressed syllable in a poem written in meter.

**Mood** The tone of a poem reflecting the author's attitudes, feelings, and perspective.

**Noun** A word that names a person, place, thing, quality, or state.

**Onomatopoeia** The formation of words that sound like or suggest the objects or actions being named.

**Parody** A comic or exaggerated imitation of a work of art.

**Personification** The assignment of human traits to things, colors, qualities, and ideas.

**Poem** A compact piece of writing containing one or more poetic elements.

**Poetic elements** The fundamentals and foundation of poetr, e.g., metaphor, simile, personification, imagery, alliteration.

**Preposition** A word that expresses a relationship between a noun, pronoun, or noun phrase and another element of the sentence.

**Repetition** (also called **anaphora**) Repeating the same words or phrases through a poem.

**Rhyme** Repetition of similar or identical sounds. **End rhyme** is rhyme at the ends of lines of a poem. **Exact rhyme** uses words with identical final sounds. **Internal rhyme** means rhyme of words within lines of a poem.

**Near rhyme** (also called **off rhyme**) uses words with similar, but not identical, sounds at the ends of words.

**Rhyme pattern** Scheme of rhyme in a poem; may occur regularly or in unique patterns.

**Traditional forms of rhyme** A **couplet** is two lines of poetry that usually rhyme. A **triplet** is a three line stanza that usually rhymes. A **quatrain** is a four line stanza usually with a set rhyme pattern. A **visual rhyme** (also called **eye rhyme**) uses words that look like, rather than sound like, they rhyme.

**Scansion** The process of marking the metrical pattern of a poem.

**Simile** A comparison between two unrelated nouns using "like" or "as" to bridge the connection.

**Sonnet** A traditional structure written in meter consisting of fourteen lines of three quatrains and a couplet.

**Stanza** A group of lines forming a structural division of a poem.

**Symbol** A sign or object representing a thing, a quality, or an idea. A **personal symbol** is a symbol significant to particular individuals or groups; has a variety of meanings. A **universal symbol** is recognized at different times in history and across cultures as having a primary or main meaning.

**Synesthesia** The description of one sense by another.

**Verb** Any class of words expressing an action performed or a state experienced by the subject. An **action verb** is a verb that shows action or motion. An **auxiliary verb** is a verb used in conjunction with another verb; a state experienced by the subject. A **linking verb** is a verb that connects the subject of the sentence to a modifier; a state experienced by the subject.

# BIBLIOGRAPHY

## General Anthologies and Resource Books

Bly, Robert. *News of the Universe, Poems of Twofold Consciousness.* Sierra Club Books, 1980.
*The Kabir Book.* The Seventies Press, Beacon Press, 1977.

Cosman, Carol; Keefe, Joan; and Weaver, Kathleen. *The Penguin Book of Women Poets.* Penguin Books, 1978.

Goldberg, Natalie. *Writing Down the Bones.* Shambhala Press, 1986.

Hugo, Richard. *The Triggering Town.* W. W. Norton & Company, 1979.

Mayes, Frances. *The Discovery of Poetry.* Harcourt Brace Jovanovich, 1987.

Mitchell, Stephen. *The Enlightened Heart.* Harper & Row, 1989.

Rexroth, Kenneth. *One Hundred Poems from the Japanese.* A New Directions Book, 1964.

Williams, Oscar. *American Verse.* Pocket Books, 1972.

Wallace, Robert. *Writing Poems.* Little, Brown and Company, 1982.
*A Poet's Journal.* Running Press, 1986.


## Children's Anthologies

Daniel, Mark. *Child's Treasury of Poems.* Dial Books, 1986.

Dunning, Stephen; Lueders, Edward; and Smith, Hugh.
    *Reflections on a Gift of Watermelon Pickle.* Scott,
    Foresman and Company, 1966.
    *Some Haystacks Don't Even Have Any Needles.*
    Lothrop, Lee and Company, 1968.

Koch, Kenneth and Kate Farrell. *Talking to the Sun.*
    Holt, Rinehart, and Winston, 1985.

Larrick, Nancy. *On City Streets.* M. Evans and Company,
    Inc., 1968.

Schenck de Regniers, Beatrice. *Sing a Song of Popcorn.*
    Scholastic Inc., 1988.

Sutherland, Zena and Arbuthnot, May Hill. *Children and
    Books.* 8th edition, HarperCollins Publishers, 1991.

## Collections by Author

Berry, Wendell. *Collected Poems.* North Point
    Press, 1985

Dickinson, Emily. *Great American Poets.*
    Clarkson N. Potter, Inc., 1986

Dylan, Bob. *Writings and Drawings.* Alfred A. Knopf,
    Inc., 1981

Ferlinghetti, Lawrence. *A Coney Island of the Mind.* New
    Directions Books, 1958.

Frost, Robert. *Collected Poems.* Henry Holt and
    Company, 1975.

Hughes, Langston. *Selected Poems.* Vintage Books, 1974.

Machado, Antonio. *Times Alone*. Wesleyan University
    Press, 1983

Oliver, Mary. *American Primitive*. Little, Brown and Company,
    1983.
    *Dream Work*. Little Brown and Company, 1986.
    *Twelve Moons*. Little Brown and Company, 1979.

Piercy, Marge. *My Mother's Body*. Alfred A. Knopf, Inc., 1985.
    *The Moon Is Always Female*. Alfred A. Knopf, Inc., 1987.
    *Stone, Paper, Knife*. Alfred A. Knopf, Inc., 1987.

Rilke, Rainier Maria. *Selected Poems*. Harper and Row
    Publishers, 1981.

Ryokan. *One Robe, One Bowl.* Weatherhill, 1988.

Rumi. *Open Secret.* Threshold Books, 1984.

Sandburg, Carl. *Complete Poems*. Harcourt Brace
    Jovanovich, 1970.

Schwartz, Alvin. *A Twister of Twists, A Tangler of
    Tongues*. J. B. Lippincott Company, 1972.

Stafford, William. *Stories That Could Be True*. Harper and
    Row Publishers, 1977.

Soseki, Muso. *Sun at Midnight*. North Point Press, 1989.

Walker, Alice. *Revolutionary Petunias and Other Poems*.
    Harcourt Brace Jovanovich, 1973.

Worth, Natalie. *all the small poems*. Farrar, Straus and
    Giroux, 1987.